T0328704

Cambridge Elements ≡

Elements in Popular Music
edited by
Rupert Till
University of Huddersfield

ROCK GUITAR VIRTUOSOS

Advances in Electric Guitar Playing, Technology, and Culture

Jan-Peter Herbst
University of Huddersfield

Alexander Paul Vallejo
Independent scholar and musician

CAMBRIDGE
UNIVERSITY PRESS

Shaftesbury Road, Cambridge CB2 8EA, United Kingdom

One Liberty Plaza, 20th Floor, New York, NY 10006, USA

477 Williamstown Road, Port Melbourne, VIC 3207, Australia

314–321, 3rd Floor, Plot 3, Splendor Forum, Jasola District Centre,
New Delhi – 110025, India

103 Penang Road, #05–06/07, Visioncrest Commercial, Singapore 238467

Cambridge University Press is part of Cambridge University Press & Assessment,
a department of the University of Cambridge.

We share the University's mission to contribute to society through the pursuit of
education, learning and research at the highest international levels of excellence.

www.cambridge.org
Information on this title: www.cambridge.org/9781009055970

DOI: 10.1017/9781009052962

First published 2023

A catalogue record for this publication is available from the British Library.

ISBN 978-1-009-05597-0 Paperback
ISSN 2634-2472 (online)
ISSN 2634-2464 (print)

Rock Guitar Virtuosos

Advances in Electric Guitar Playing, Technology, and Culture

Elements in Popular Music

DOI: 10.1017/9781009052962
First published online: November 2023

Jan-Peter Herbst
University of Huddersfield

Alexander Paul Vallejo
Independent scholar and musician

Author for correspondence: Jan-Peter Herbst, j.herbst@hud.ac.uk

Abstract: The guitar has been an integral part of popular music and mainstream culture for many decades and in many places of the world. This Element examines the development and current state of virtuosic rock guitar in terms of playing, technology, and culture. Supported by technological advances such as extended-range guitars, virtuosos in the twenty-first century are exploring ways to expand standard playing techniques in a climate where ever-higher levels of perfection are expected. As musician-entrepreneurs, contemporary rock guitar virtuosos record, produce, and market their music themselves; operate equipment companies; and sell merchandise, tablature, and lessons online. For their social media channels, they regularly create videos and interact with their followers while having to balance building their tribe and finding the time to develop their craft to stay competitive. For a virtuoso, working situations have changed considerably since the last century; the aloof rock star has been replaced by the approachable virtuoso-guitarist-composer-innovator-producer-promoter-YouTuber-teacher-entrepreneur.

Keywords: virtuosity, electric guitar, rock music, metal music, technology

ISBNs: 9781009055970 (PB), 9781009052962 (OC)
ISSNs: 2634-2472 (online), 2634-2464 (print)

Contents

1 Introduction

For several decades, if not centuries, and in many parts of the world, the guitar has been an integral part of popular music and mainstream culture (Dawe, 2010). It became an idolised instrument with its electrification (Waksman, 1999), followed by the rock'n'roll boom in the 1950s and the subsequent diversification of rock music into hard rock, psychedelic rock, and heavy metal. Mass fabrication from the 1960s and 1970s onwards made guitars and amplifiers more accessible (Kraft, 2004) and paved the way for aspiring guitarists, resulting in a wealth of hard rock and heavy metal bands from the 1980s onwards. In the 1990s, the guitar was fundamental in the mainstream genres of grunge, indie rock, and nu metal. Since the turn of the millennium, new ways of using the instrument have been explored in the subgenres of rock and metal, as well as other forms of popular music.

Speculation that the heyday of the guitar is fading came from Eric Clapton, who mused in 2017 that 'maybe the guitar is over' (Bliss, 2017), and from an article in *The Washington Post* predicting the 'slow, secret death of the six-string electric' (Edgers, 2017). Such rumours have circulated since at least the 1990s (Rotundi, 1997). Some genres of popular music are created entirely on the computer, without use of physical instruments, and it is fair to say that this trend has caused the guitar to lose much of its presence on mainstream radio. Nevertheless, numerous scenes and communities of the electric guitar defy this development. Journalist Rob Copsey (2019) points out that guitar sales have more than doubled in the last decade, reaching their highest number in history. Guitar.com concurs: 'the guitar is not dead, the guitar is thriving' (*Guitar.com,* 2019).

Some researchers and practitioners share the mainstream media's pessimistic view of the electric guitar. James Slaven and Jodi Krout conclude from their musicological analysis that, while guitar solos became ever faster between the 1950s and the 2000s, the 'general techniques of guitar soloing have changed very little since the beginnings of the rock era in the 1950s, even though the style of playing has seen dramatic changes' (Slaven & Krout, 2016: 246). They further argue that most of the early rock techniques had already been used by guitarists since the late nineteenth century and were common even earlier on other string instruments, such as the violin. In a similar vein, solo artist and guitar educator Joe Stump claims that whilst 'metal/shred guitar has evolved and changed in all kinds of ways over the years, many of these techniques have remained constant' (Stump, 2014: 94). There is some truth to these statements, but what these authors fail to address is that electric guitar techniques have developed over time, sometimes enabling novel forms of expression such as percussive thumping and polyphonic multi-role eight-finger tapping. Furthermore, neither the academic nor the educational literature offers any explanation as to how speed has increased over the decades.

This Element was motivated by speculation about stagnation in electric guitar playing and a lack of academic recognition of advances since Eddie Van Halen reconfigured the instrument on Van Halen's debut album in 1978 (Walser, 1992: 276). Even in contemporary guitar manuals for aspiring virtuosos, 1980s guitarists are still treated as 'state of the art'. While it is acknowledged that rock guitarists from the 1980s have superseded virtuosos of the 1970s such as Ritchie Blackmore and Uli Jon Roth in terms of playing speed and precision, little consideration has been given to developments and innovative players in the twenty-first century. Our analysis of why particular guitarists became widely recognised and joined the established canons, as evidenced by educational material and greatest lists, and how they advanced the instrument will make the case that electric guitar playing has continued to evolve.

We will examine how rock guitarists searching for new forms of expression, ever higher speeds, and virtuosity dealt with the ergonomics of the instrument. Exploring playing techniques requires cultural, social, medial, and economic contexts. After all, cultural change, advances in guitar and amplification technology, recording practices, and showmanship led to the emergence of the rock guitar heroes of the 1960s (Millard, 2004a; Weinstein, 2013). Any analysis of the development of electric guitar playing must therefore consider issues of culture, technology, production, the recording industry, income streams, and the musical zeitgeist to understand how playing reflects and drives cultural change. This includes how culture is passed on, how music is released, and how guitarists form specialist communities.

First, however, virtuosity must be discussed to place the virtuosic rock guitar scenes in a broader tradition. The virtuosity debate in music reached a climax during the Classical and Romantic periods in the eighteenth and nineteenth centuries. Virtuosity culminated in the technically demanding playing and extravagant performances of nineteenth-century icons such as Niccolò Paganini and Franz Liszt, who set the scene for the guitar virtuosos to come. The term 'virtuoso' was originally associated with theorists and composers but was gradually applied to performers with exceptional technical abilities, artistry, and showmanship (Ginsborg, 2018: 455). Although novelty and progress have generally been regarded as beneficial to creative practice in Western societies (Niu & Sternberg, 2006), virtuosity was frequently reduced to the pursuit of higher speeds, sacrificing music's expressive and emotional qualities (Stachó, 2018; Wood, 2010). Virtuosity has been divisive. Opponents have accused virtuosos of selfishness and indulgence, showing off their playing skills or persona, and putting the self before collective ensemble performance (Frith, 2007: 325). The one-sided focus on technique as an end in itself with little musical value has been a constant point of criticism in classical and popular music (Frith, 2007; Wood, 2010). Since Liszt, and especially in recent history with the metal guitar hero (Fellezs, 2018: 118; Walser, 1992: 300), musicians have provoked condemnation with their extravagant displays of technical prowess. But virtuosity is not only aesthetically controversial; it also poses practical problems with ethical implications. Excellence is required of professional musicians, and perfection has merely become the 'starting-point before other kinds of virtuosity come into play' (Leech-Wilkinson, 2018: 558–9).

Advocates of virtuosity have long argued that technical skill and expressiveness are mutually dependent, as technique is merely the ability to realise artistic visions and feelings as authentically as possible (Stachó, 2018: 540). Moreover, musical development needs the sounding out and shifting of boundaries, and it requires an element of virtuosity, one that is motivated by a 'musical urge' (Hennion, 2012: 126). While virtuosity can benefit musical development in general, it is necessary to advance both the instrument and the music played with it. Virtuosos may therefore contribute to musical development, especially in more progressive forms of music.

The shift from composition to interpretation has added to the controversy of virtuosity. In classical aesthetics, the genius in music is in the written composition. The nineteenth-century virtuoso embellished the score and rose above the composer, reversing the traditional hierarchy (Wood, 2010) and showing that performance can be as fascinating and aesthetically valuable as the composition itself. For music sociologist Antoine Hennion (2012: 129), such fascination takes two forms. Audiences may be fascinated by what they hear or cannot believe they are hearing, like the fascination a magician evokes. Novelty is enjoyable because it breaks with convention and offers new experiences. To maintain this sensation, the presentation must progress. Publications such as *The Guinness Book of Records* suggest that people find it exciting to see how fields of practice strive for new heights. The second kind of fascination is the spectacle of humans becoming automatons – that is, humans performing music with machine-like perfection. Musicologist Michael Custodis (2017: 49) explains the longstanding popularity of the progressive metal band Dream Theater with precisely this kind of fascination. The band manages to capture music on the record that is so fast, technical, and awkward to play that one might imagine it is written with little consideration of how humans might perform it. As anthropologist Anya Royce (2004: 18–19) points out, virtuosity and speed are only a problem when used for their own sake. That may not be the case with Dream Theater, whose virtuosity is fundamental to their artistic concept and main appeal (Custodis, 2017).

The evaluation of virtuosity has become more complex over time. As Hennion (2012: 126) notes, a duality of technique and expression has increasingly become over-simplistic in times of musical cross-pollination. In her study of what virtuosity means to classical musicians, musicologist Jane Ginsborg (2018: 471) finds that most players see it as a tool for music-making and adopt a more relativist stance by avoiding value judgements. They instead embrace stylistic versatility for musical reasons, which requires virtuosity. Many of the guitar-centred rock bands and artists that have emerged in the last decade use virtuosity similarly for stylistic, expressive, and creative purposes.

Several guitarists covered in this Element have advanced musical genres, playing styles, and instrument design. Early rock guitar heroes of the 1960s and 1970s explored the potential of distortion and effects in rock music and how the lead guitar could employ a distorted sound to create a style outside the idioms of the blues. The 1980s and 1990s were decades dedicated to the pursuit of speed and progress in playing techniques. Much criticism and appeal to virtuosity concerned the shred guitar style of this era. The 1990s and 2000s were characterised by experimentation with sound effects, seven-string guitars, and more modern amplifiers. After the shred boom, advances in guitar playing were grounded in bridging styles and genres. Inspired by other instruments, guitarists explored new affordances of techniques and technologies not only for their instrument but also for songwriting, recording, and production. Changes in music technology include extended-range guitars with seven or more strings, a break with the decades-long dominance of valve-based analogue amplifiers, widespread availability of digital recording and production resources, and Web 2.0 providing a medium for connecting guitarists around the world. The relevance of digital communities can hardly be overstated since they allow players to share their ideas with fellow musicians and bypass gatekeepers such as record labels. This development has allowed contemporary players to inspire others and make a living as virtuosos from their homes.

The guitar in rock and popular music has been important in mainstream musical culture, but guitarists have also always formed specialist communities to discuss subject-specific topics related to playing, gear, and trends. We can understand such specialist groups as 'communities of practice' (Wenger, 1998) with guitar playing and culture at their core. Members do not know the entire community, but they need to understand the unwritten rules and common knowledge within the group, which in the case of guitarists includes influential players past and present, epochal moments, and shared values.

We believe there can be no definitive historiography of virtuosic rock guitar playing because too many subjective variables and value judgements would be involved. Following the concept of 'communities of practice' (Wenger, 1998), we draw on our experiences as members of guitar communities and analyse their discourse as reflected in the written and unwritten canons found in guitar compendia, greatest lists, teaching materials such as guitar handbooks, and other sources on the Internet (see Section 2). Methodologically, we are guided by qualitative media analysis (Altheide & Schneider, 2013; Bowen, 2009), also known as ethnographic content analysis (Altheide & Schneider, 2013: 5). This method is suitable for understanding culture, social discourse, and social change through documents created and received in the scene, such as magazines, websites, and audio-visual materials (Bowen, 2009). Naturally, media like guitar magazines such as *Guitar World* are selective and favour some artists while neglecting others, but they are opinion-forming and must therefore be taken seriously. By choosing an ethnographic method of studying popular media, our analysis of the development of virtuosic rock guitar playing and culture must consequently be understood as a capture of popular discourse, which cannot claim complete historical accuracy and coverage of artists and developments. However, given the relative lack of research on contemporary guitar playing (see Dawe, 2010), our approach of combining analysis of popular discourse with our own observations as insiders is a first step in filling in the gaps in a guitar scholarship that has neglected advances in playing style and technique since the 1990s.

The starting point of our investigation is establishing canons of electric guitar virtuosos through a meta-analysis of handbooks, greatest lists, and guitar compendia (Section 2). In so doing, we determine performative and aesthetic criteria for the inclusion in the canons over more than fifty years of electric guitar playing. Section 3 introduces the electric guitar's main playing techniques. The three subsequent sections study the evolution of electric guitar playing with many noteworthy artists. We begin with the first generation of rock guitar heroes, who laid the foundation for virtuosity in rock music and the instrumental solo artist (Section 4). The discussion includes the introduction of neoclassical shred, innovation in instrument design, and playing techniques such as tapping, sound effects, and recording techniques. Subsequently, the canonical rock guitar virtuosos and shredders of the 1980s to the 2000s are explored (Section 5). This section identifies reasons why players joined the canons, covering characteristics such as influence, feel and expressiveness, versatility, knowledge of harmony and theory, performative and production aspects, and educational products. Next, stylistic, musical, and technological developments in the twenty-first century are investigated (Section 6). Our analysis suggests that playing has incorporated new techniques and that virtuosos use their technical skills for rhythm guitar and songwriting. This is apparent from their exploration of rhythmic techniques such as bass guitar-inspired thumping or two-handed multi-finger tapping used for piano-like accompaniment rather than lead guitar. Finally, shifting the focus away from playing, we examine the current guitar scene, with its income streams that allow virtuosos to make a living (Section 7). Some of today's best-known players in the scene have hardly released music through traditional channels, relying instead on video platforms and social media.

2 Establishing a Canon

This section creates a framework for analysing the development of rock guitar playing and the respective guitar scenes, as depicted in popular discourse. After discussing the significance and cultural power of canons, we determine a canon of relevant guitarists between the 1960s and the present day, based on the discourse observable in guitar handbooks and journalistic lists of the greatest guitarists.

2.1 The Canon and Its Value

Canon research is well established in education and in disciplines such as literary and religious studies. In music, canons also provide a valuable tool for analysing dominant values, socio-demographic structures, and conflicts of power (Appen & Doehring, 2006; Citron, 1993; Jones, 2017; Regev, 2006). A canon is usually a collection of musical content. Albums have become canonical because they are 'supposedly the undisputed "masterpieces" . . . and typically presented as peaks of the aesthetic power of the art form in question, as ultimate manifestations of aesthetic perfection, complexity of form and depth of expression' (Regev, 2006: 1). Such works and the artists associated with them are recognised as significant in their field; they are formally embedded in culture and exercise cultural power. The works and what they represent are passed on in educational curricula (Guillory, 2010; Wendell, 1991). In less formal settings, canonical artists are included in compendia, rankings, and greatest lists.

As part of cultural history, canons reduce a field to its essence (Jones, 2017: 7). However, the selection of notable works and artists is sometimes not based on purely aesthetic merit but motivated by interests in conveying idealistic values (Corse & Griffin, 1997: 174–5). Canon formation can therefore also be understood as a 'scene of competition for the power to grant cultural consecration' (Bourdieu, 1985: 25) and as an instrument of social control and exclusion (Anderson & Zanetti, 2000: 345). A canon represents a site of conflict between past genius and present aspirations. Canons are consistently being challenged and, over time, show the evolution of artists and works deemed important (Jones, 2017: 8). As much as canons dictate and possibly distort the historical narrative, they represent development and have the potential to inspire creativity in the future (Regev, 2006: 2).

There is no single form of canon. Literary scholar Alastair Fowler (1979: 98–9) distinguishes between the selective and the critical canon; the first consists of lists in anthologies, the second of works repeatedly treated in articles and books. The two overlap insofar as the critical canon is composed of selective canons. Harris Wendell (1991: 113) differentiates between a relatively stable diachronic canon and the rapidly changing canon, from which only some works enter the diachronic canon. That is why several canons exist at the same time, interacting with each other. While some remain relatively constant, others reflect the current state of the art. Canons have adapted to the diverse subcultures and plurality of today's lifestyles. In most fields of practice, there is still a canon for the greatest works of all time, but smaller canons for more specialised art forms provide structure in a complex world (Jones, 2017: 1).

Canons are rarely directly accessible but implicit in books and curricula. By contrast, a list is explicit. It is the overt but simplified form of the canon (Kenner, 1984: 373). Compilation lists as shorthand manifestations of canons provide clues to a 'microcosm of values' (Jones, 2017: 26) and information about the greatest artists and works. These have been central to music journalism for decades when discussing the best records of all time, the last year, or a recent month. The number of compilation lists has multiplied with the proliferation of the Internet. Who selects the work is unchanged; in both print and online, it can be editors, other experts in the field, the readership, or a mixture of these. The constitution of the voting members, their interests and motives, and their age structure have an impact on the list, with younger readers often favouring more recent music over established works (Jones, 2017: 94, 122).

The selection criteria reveal values in the field of practice. The overarching criterion in music is *originality* (Jones, 2017: 17; Talbot, 2000: 3–5). Canonical works stand out from preceding and other contemporary works. Originality includes features such as strangeness, weirdness, or the extraordinary portrayal of the familiar that makes works unique and potentially influential (Jones, 2017: 17). Another criterion related to originality is *timelessness* (Jones, 2017: 9; Kermode, 1985: 62–90). Works that pass the test of time are called masterpieces and likely appeal to a younger audience, too (Appen & Doehring, 2006: 22). A third criterion is *complexity* because multidimensional works offer the potential for discussion and ongoing engagement (Jones, 2017: 17). *Virtuosity* is a controversial criterion in musical canons. Aesthetic value is generally regarded as superior to practical, sentimental, or hedonistic value. Hence, complexity and greatness in composition and arrangement are preferred to a mere display of virtuosic technique (Jones, 2017: 15). However, good virtuosity is defined by technical skills used for the sake of originality (Heister, 2004: 17). Since virtuosity can be grounded in imagination, thereby leading to creativity and innovation (Leech-Wilkinson, 2018: 560), it potentially fulfils the two criteria of originality and complexity so that virtuosity may be positively judged if it suits the music.

2.2 The Canons of Electric Guitar Heroes and Virtuosos

A canon is seldom clearly visible. To extract various relevant canons of guitar virtuosos, we analysed two forms of data: thirty guitar handbooks and thirty greatest lists (see Appendix). All sources were systematically examined to extrapolate which players are mentioned and for what they are known. This information guides the analysis of the development of rock guitar playing in later sections.

As one of the more formal manifestations of the canon, handbooks are representative of the educational curriculum and can be considered their own canon. Despite having reduced relevance due to the rise of online learning resources, handbooks retain their influence in educational settings and are more accessible for the study of discourse than scattered video tutorials and online lessons. Greatest lists are a simplified and condensed form of the canon and provide useful information about core values and the contribution of specific players to the guitar community (Jones, 2017: 26; Kenner, 1984: 373). Such lists offer aesthetic guidance by indicating 'who deserves to be in the pantheon and what is worthy to emulate' (Weinstein, 2013: 149). In the context of guitarists, it must be noted that the various canons differ from most other art canons in that it is not so much a specific release being recognised but a player's style.

Guitar Handbooks

The canon of guitar manuals was determined by analysing thirty handbooks on electric guitar technique and shred guitar playing with an average publication date of 2013. Table 1 shows the percentage of books wherein specific guitarists are mentioned. The absolute numbers are not considered because one book (Brooks, 2017) is dedicated solely to Yngwie Malmsteen, which would skew the distribution. The relative percentage of references made to a guitarist in handbooks is thus a way to evaluate recognition of a player's technique and its creative use.

The list given in Table 1 suggests that most of the featured guitarists are rock and metal players. This can partly be explained by the books analysed, several of which are for metal lead guitar. However, even in those books not focused on a specific genre, rock and metal artists dominate, with some notable exceptions

Table 1 Reference to players in guitar handbooks

Rank	Player	Percentage
1	Yngwie Malmsteen	85%
2	Paul Gilbert	69%
3	Joe Satriani / Steve Vai / Eddie Van Halen	58%
6	John Petrucci	54%
7	Randy Rhoads	46%
8	Jason Becker / Frank Gambale / Vinnie More	42%
11	Ritchie Blackmore / Al Di Meola / Greg Howe	38%
14	Marty Friedman / Uli Jon Roth	35%
16	Michael Angelo Batio / 'Dimebag' Darrell / Steve Morse	31%
19	Jimi Hendrix / Allan Holdsworth / Shawn Lane / George Lynch / Michael Romeo / Zakk Wylde	27%
25	Guthrie Govan / Kirk Hammett / Jeff Loomis / John McLaughlin	23%
29	Nuno Bettencourt / Brett Garsed / Eric Johnson / Tony MacAlpine / Gary Moore	19%
34	Reb Beach / Buckethead / Mattias Eklundh / Stanley Jordan / Richie Kotzen / Michael Schenker	15%
40	Tosin Abasi / Jennifer Batten / Rusty Cooley	12%
43	Warren Di Martini / Alexi Laiho / Josh Martin / Tom Morello / Dave Mustaine / Andy Timmons	8%

for fusion players such as Allan Holdsworth, John McLaughlin, and Frank Gambale.

Several players are less widely known, indicating a guitar-specific canon outside the popular music mainstream. Some of them appear in other canons for their roles in successful bands, such as Paul Gilbert and Richie Kotzen in Mr. Big, Marty Friedman in Megadeth, George Lynch in Dokken, Nuno Bettencourt in Extreme, and Reb Beach in Winger. These examples have in common that they are hard rock and metal bands primarily popular in the 1980s and 1990s. The same is true for many of the listed players. Most gained popularity as members of popular bands or solo artists in the 1980s, some with continued success in the 1990s and later. Only two players active from the 2000s are on the list of featured players: Animals as Leaders' Tosin Abasi and Little Tybee's Josh Martin. The data suggests that guitar handbooks focus on long-established guitarists and their approaches to techniques but tend to overlook contemporary guitarists.

Greatest Lists

The guitar handbooks discuss players mostly in terms of their technical ability and less for their popularity and creativity. In contrast, some lists of the greatest guitarists disclose a broader set of selection criteria, indicating values appreciated in the electric guitar communities. Concurring with the previous deliberations (see Section 2.1), influence, originality, and technical skill are the main criteria, with influence holding the greatest weight (Kitts & Tolinski, 2002: 1–2). Influence is specified through reference to innovation, pushing boundaries (McIver, 2008: 8–9), exciting imagination, changing the way we approach the instrument (Turner & Rubin, 2020), overall impact on the guitar scene, and level of success (Bienstock, 2019c). Several sources acknowledge the development of playing in the last two decades, speak of a 'golden age in the guitar world', and emphasise that young players with developed skills emerging from the underground are ahead of their 'elders and betters' (McIver, 2008: 9). While virtuosity has sometimes been connoted negatively (Frith, 2007; Wood, 2010), it seems to be a positive trademark in certain electric guitar communities and is seen as conducive to musical progress. Guitar scholar André Millard even regards virtuosity as a prerequisite for the rock guitar hero, necessary to lead the instrument into 'new dimensions' and define it in new ways for which the hero is appreciated and emulated (Millard, 2004a: 143–4).

We divided the total sample of the thirty greatest lists from 2002 to 2020 with an average publication date of 2017 into smaller meta-lists because they cannot be compared directly and represent different rock guitar sub-canons. Due to the different numbering formats of the individual lists, we distinguished only between inclusion and non-inclusion and did not weigh the rankings. Guided by the handbooks and due to the scope of this Element, we only considered players classified as virtuosos in the selection.

The meta-list of the greatest and most influential players (Table 2) contains many of the same names as the previous list derived from handbooks. The main difference lies in the ranking, with Jimi Hendrix, Eddie Van Halen, Ritchie Blackmore, and Randy Rhoads at the top of the list of greatest players. Even fifty years after his passing, Hendrix tops most lists, demonstrating his significant contribution to the instrument. Van Halen is included for his original and virtuosic approach to soloing that has inspired generations of guitarists, as well as his contribution to the instrument's design and amplification. Blackmore is acknowledged as the 'father of neoclassical metal and shred guitar' (Sulem, 2020). Yngwie Malmsteen is also best known for his technique. Amongst the players mentioned in the handbooks but not included in any of the greatest lists are Frank Gambale, Vinnie Moore, Greg Howe, and Michael Angelo Batio.

Table 2 Meta-list of the greatest and most influential guitar players

Rank	Player	Percentage
1	Jimi Hendrix / Eddie Van Halen	100%
3	Ritchie Blackmore / Randy Rhoads	80%
5	Joe Satriani	67%
6	Steve Vai	60%
7	'Dimebag' Darrell / Yngwie Malmsteen / Tom Morello	53%
10	Paul Gilbert / Kirk Hammett / John McLaughlin / Gary Moore	40%
14	Zakk Wylde	33%
15	Al Di Meola / Eric Johnson / Steve Morse / John Petrucci	27%
19	Allan Holdsworth	20%
20	Nuno Bettencourt / Buckethead / Guthrie Govan / Steve Lukather / George Lynch / Dave Mustaine / Uli Jon Roth	13%
27	Tosin Abasi / Jason Becker / Alexi Laiho / Misha Mansoor	7%

$n = 15$ lists

However, others included in the list of greatest guitarists are also known for their virtuosity and technique, such as Joe Satriani, Steve Vai, John McLaughlin, and Allan Holdsworth.

Several fusion players active since the late 1960s inspired influential virtuosos such as Eddie Van Halen, Joe Satriani, John Petrucci, Yngwie Malmsteen, and Tom Morello. John McLaughlin has had a lasting influence on virtuosos through his fusion of jazz and rock music, captured on his instrumental solo guitar albums. He is mostly known for his rock-inspired, fast, and intense alternate picking of jazz licks (*Guitar World*, 2015). The same applies to Al Di Meola, who combines quick and precise alternate-picked scale runs with elements of rock, classical, and flamenco guitar (Kitts & Tolinski, 2002: 42). Unlike McLaughlin and Di Meola, Allan Holdsworth is known primarily for his fluid and fast legato technique (Govan, 2002a: 110).

Players who began their careers in the twenty-first century are rarely included in the lists; only Tosin Abasi and Misha Mansoor represent the current generation of guitarists. Other than Deep Purple, Ozzy Osbourne, Van Halen, and Metallica, many players are either members of lesser-known bands or solo artists, suggesting that the electric guitar scenes differ from mainstream popular music. Most of the lesser-known names gained visibility in the guitar scene through their releases on Shrapnel Records, a driving force for shred guitar in the 1980s and 1990s.

The meta-list of greatest metal players (Table 3) widely coincides with the list of greatest players of all time (Table 2). Former Pantera guitarist 'Dimebag' Darrell Lance Abbott is included in all lists for being 'one of the most influential metal guitarists of the 90s' (McIver, 2008: 191) and the 'premier metal guitarist of the new millennium' (Kitts & Tolinski, 2002: 13). Mention is made of his various musical influences, including blues and country; his mastery of standard playing techniques that he used for expressive playing; his rhythmic abilities and groove; and the virtuosity he kept alive in 1990s rock music when grunge threatened virtuosic guitar culture (Lalaina, 2008; Wiederhorn, 2015). The players listed second seem to have achieved their ranking mainly because of their influence as members of famous bands: for example, Randy Rhoads and Zakk Wylde in Ozzy Osbourne's band and Kirk Hammett in Metallica. Band membership alone would probably not have bestowed them this ranking had their playing not also been influential. Hammett popularised playing with the wah-wah effect and showed new generations of guitarists that blues elements can be mixed with thrash metal (Sulem, 2020). Rhoads incorporated classical influences into metal music, and Wylde added blues and country elements to the metal sound. Compared to former Megadeth colleague and respected virtuoso Marty Friedman, Dave Mustaine is an oddity. Selected as the best player in rock journalist Joel McIver's (2008) list of the 100 greatest metal guitarists, his trademark is fast playing with basic techniques rather than virtuosic use of advanced techniques such as sweeping and tapping, as was common in the 1980s (*Guitar Metrics*, 2020). Another unusual guitarist is Tom Morello, whose development of a new sonic vocabulary through pedals and sound effects

Table 3 Meta-list of the greatest metal players

Rank	Player	Percentage
1	'Dimebag' Darrell	100%
2	Kirk Hammett / Randy Rhoads / Zakk Wylde	80%
5	Marty Friedman / Synyster Gates / George Lynch / Tom Morello / Dave Mustaine / Alex Skolnick	60%
11	Nuno Bettencourt / Alexi Laiho / Jeff Loomis / Yngwie Malmsteen / John Petrucci / Michael Romeo	40%
17	Michael Angelo Batio / Jason Becker / Ritchie Blackmore / Paul Gilbert / Tony MacAlpine / Vinnie Moore / Uli Jon Roth / Joe Satriani / Eddie Van Halen	20%

n = 5 lists

influenced players in the 1990s and 2000s (*Rolling Stone*, 2015). Synyster Gates, guitarist of Avenged Sevenfold, is the only contemporary player on the list. He is credited with having introduced 'Generation Y to the shock and awe of a brilliant guitar solo' (*Guitar World*, 2015).

The meta-list of virtuosos and shredders (Table 4) reads like a mixture of the greatest players of all time (Table 2) and the greatest metal players (Table 3), which supports the impression that virtuosos are viewed positively in the guitar community. Paul Gilbert, Yngwie Malmsteen, Joe Satriani, and Steve Vai are included in every list. They all have characteristic features: Malmsteen took neoclassical metal to another level; Gilbert fused shred guitar with his penchant for kitschy pop music; and Satriani and Vai helped make the instrumental guitar album a category of its own in the 1980s and 1990s. The players ranked second are noteworthy too. As a solo artist and member of the 1980s metal band Cacophony, Jason Becker is described as the 'titan of neoclassical shredding' (*Guitar World*, 2015). He is included in most lists even though he only released three albums in 1987 and 1988 before contracting amyotrophic lateral sclerosis (ALS). Buckethead is better known for playing in Guns N' Roses between 2000 and 2004 than for his virtuosic solo albums that blend rock and metal with jazz, funk, ambient, and avant-garde (*Loudwire*, 2016). His output is noteworthy given his 31 full-length albums and 283 mini-albums with a runtime of 30 minutes, of which he released 118 within one year (2015). Guitarist John

Table 4 Meta-list of virtuosos and shredders

Rank	Player	Percentage
1	Paul Gilbert / Yngwie Malmsteen / Joe Satriani / Steve Vai	100%
5	Jason Becker / Buckethead	80%
7	Michael Angelo Batio / Greg Howe / Eric Johnson / Richie Kotzen / Jeff Loomis / John Petrucci / Eddie Van Halen	60%
14	Nuno Bettencourt / Al Di Meola / Marty Friedman / Chris Impellitteri / Shawn Lane / George Lynch / Tony MacAlpine / Vinnie Moore / Steve Morse / Randy Rhoads / Uli Jon Roth / Alex Skolnick	40%
26	Tosin Abasi / Ritchie Blackmore / 'Dimebag' Darrell / Frank Gambale / Synyster Gates / Guthrie Govan / Allan Holdsworth / Alexi Laiho / John McLaughlin / Polyphia / Zakk Wylde	20%

n = 5 lists

Petrucci of the progressive metal band Dream Theater remains the 'most celebrated and popular guitarist in the world of progressive metal' (Bienstock, 2019c), even after thirty years on the guitar scene, due to his technical command, sense of melody, and exploration of new sounds. Contemporary players included are Tosin Abasi, Synyster Gates, and (collectively) Polyphia guitarists Scott LePage and Timothy Henson. Polyphia's ranking is due to the fact that their guitarists use their technical abilities for unusual and memorable melodies rather than fast shredding (*Total Guitar*, 2020).

The meta-list of newcomers and notable players of the last decade (Table 5) comprises a mixture of established and newer players. Veterans of instrumental guitar music Joe Satriani and Steve Vai are still listed. Although Vai has released only three studio albums in the last twenty years, *Guitar World* acknowledges his 'dominant presence in the guitar landscape' (Bienstock, 2019c) and notes him as a constant figure in the scene. Satriani is recognised for his ability to transcend eras and remain relevant by continuing to 'innovate the way guitarists perform today with its techno and modern feel' (Ear to the Ground Music) and his 'extraordinary and envelope-pushing' work (Bienstock, 2019c). Guthrie Govan is another experienced player to whom similar criteria apply. He 'managed to find fresh inspiration and adapt to changing musical fashions' (Bitoun, 2018: 234) with his band The Aristocrats and as guitarist in Steven Wilson's band. Nicknamed 'Professor Shred', he is 'one of the most mind-blowing and versatile players on the scene today, with a ridiculously fast and fluid technique' (Bienstock, 2019c).

The newer players on the list suggest that the electric guitar community is becoming increasingly diverse, not only in socio-demographic terms but also regarding music release formats. Some guitarists play in traditional bands; others are solo artists, producing music and guitar videos at home. One such example is guitar virtuoso and social media master Mateus Asato, described as the 'Kim Kardashian of instrumental guitar' (Bienstock, 2019c), with a fan base

Table 5 Meta-list of newcomers and notable players of the last decade

Rank	Player	Percentage
1	Mateus Asato	80%
2	Plini / Jason Richardson	60%
4	Tosin Abasi / Guthrie Govan / Scott LePage / Kiko Loureiro / Misha Mansoor / Joe Satriani / Nita Strauss / Yvette Young	40%
12	Synyster Gates / Sarah Longfield / Ichika Nito / John Petrucci / Steve Vai	20%

n = 5 lists

of one million Instagram followers and 335,000 subscribers to his YouTube channel despite having never released an album (*Guitar.com,* 2019). Asato plays neo-soul with a sophisticated chord-melody fingerstyle (Sidwell, 2018; *Total Guitar,* 2020). The second rank is shared by Plini and Jason Richardson, two progressive rock and metal artists. While Plini utilises his technical skills for melodic compositions, dreamy chord progressions, and immersive sound-scapes (*Guitar.com,* 2019; Sidwell, 2018), Richardson belongs to the new generation of metal shredders, with fast and precise technique, as presented on his solo album and guest appearances on other releases (Bienstock, 2019c). Misha Mansoor of the djent metal band Periphery has been a driving force in popularising extended-range guitars and remains a mainstay of the contempor-ary guitar world (Bienstock, 2019c). Tosin Abasi is similarly described as one of the 'world's greatest innovators' (*Ear To The Ground Music,* 2020), transform-ing the eight-string guitar into a new medium for melody and rhythm playing (Bienstock, 2019c). Kiko Loureiro receives attention as Megadeth's latest lead guitarist, enriching the band's sound with an 'energized and utterly unique approach – precision-picked, incredibly fast and fluid licks studded with unusual phrasings, exotic scales and expressive note bends' (Bienstock, 2019c). In his solo releases, he mixes progressive metal with Brazilian influ-ences such as bossa nova and samba. Another social media master is Van Halen-inspired Ichika Nito, who uses finger tapping to create pianistic rhythms and melody lines (*Total Guitar,* 2020).

The electric guitar community has long been dominated by male, white players from North America and Central Europe. The meta-list indicates a gradual change. It includes three women who represent a much larger number of female players in the contemporary scene. The most visible of the three is Nita Strauss, a successful solo artist and touring guitarist for Alice Cooper. She is described as 'the very definition of a guitar hero in the modern age' (*Total Guitar,* 2020) and a populariser of contemporary shred (Bienstock, 2019c). Yvette Young, a solo artist and frontwoman of the math-rock band Covet, is highlighted for her virtuosic tapping technique, inspired by her classical piano and violin training (*Guitar.com,* 2019). The YouTube solo artist Sarah Longfield, who has released three studio albums and six EPs, is also recognised for her original approach to tapping (*Total Guitar,* 2020) and extended-range guitar playing.

The handbooks and lists of greatest guitarists suggest that originality, expres-siveness, emotional playing, and technical ability are not the only prerequisites for entering a canon. The most acknowledged players use virtuosity to advance music and carve space for unique styles and personalities, and many offer qualities beyond technique. As solo artists and band members, lead and rhythm guitar players, composers and sometimes producers, they are more than just automatons that mindlessly reproduce music. They may not be known to the mainstream, but they influence contemporary guitar scenes through their online activities and social media engagement.

3 Overview of Electric Guitar Playing Techniques

Analysing virtuosic playing requires the description of guitar-specific techniques. This section introduces techniques and the corresponding notation particular to the electric guitar. Since writing about the ergonomics of playing techniques is like dancing about architecture, to adapt a famous quote, we have produced several videos to help illustrate the techniques through demonstration (see YouTube playlist in the Appendix).

Playing techniques for the electric guitar can be roughly divided into four categories: picking, legato, harmonic, and percussive. Picking and legato are the two main techniques, with picking referring to all articulation using a plectrum (also called a pick) to excite the string and legato pertaining to techniques without a plectrum. Picked notes sound defined and hard, while legato phrasing is fluid. Percussive articulation is not as clearly defined. It includes techniques such as muting strings to create a rhythmic sound without a pitch, as well as bass-inspired slapping techniques to play notes with a percussive sound quality. Harmonic techniques are similarly varied, ranging from picking and legato to percussive excitation of the string. The main difference is the dominant presence of harmonic overtones that creates a hollow, bell-like sound.

Picking comprises several techniques, all based on downstrokes (tablature notation: ⊓) and upstrokes (∨). Playing downstrokes produces the most accentuated sound while being limited in speed. The tempo can be doubled with *alternate picking*: alternating downstrokes and upstrokes (Figure 1).

As it is a systematic approach, alternate picking can be used for any melody. However, when notes are played on adjacent strings, other picking techniques are better suited. *Sweep picking*, for example, allows one note per string to be played with a continuous, strum-like motion (Figure 2).

Sweeping avoids the challenges of alternate picking posed in arpeggio-based motifs. It decreases the number of times a lower string is picked with a downstroke and a higher with an upstroke, which is called *outside picking* and involves a large picking motion (Figure 3). Sweeping further prevents being trapped between strings when a higher string is played with a downstroke followed by a lower one with an upstroke, a mechanism called *inside picking* (Figure 3).

Figure 1 Alternate picking of a pentatonic scale

Figure 2 Arpeggio motif involving sweep picking

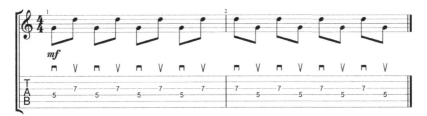

Figure 3 Outside (left) and inside (right) picking

Sweep picking is the most ergonomic method for phrases with single notes on adjacent strings. If a phrase contains a different number of notes per string, a mixture of alternate and sweep picking may be used, known as *economy picking*. This differs from alternate picking in that the pick direction always follows the most direct path (Figure 4).

All picking techniques can be combined with *palm muting* (PM), an articulation in which the picking hand is placed on the played string to muffle the sound (Figure 5). Palm-muting allows changing articulation within a phrase or improving rhythmic clarity by shortening note lengths.

Legato also consists of several techniques involving little or no use of the pick. There are four core mechanics: hammer-on, pull-off, tapping, and slide. The *hammer-on* (∩) involves playing a note on a string by tapping the finger with force on the fretboard. It is often combined with the *pull-off*

Figure 4 Economy picking of a blues pentatonic scale

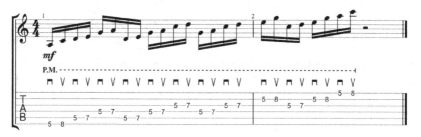

Figure 5 Palm-muted alternate picking of a pentatonic sequence

Figure 6 Pull-off and hammer-on legato phrase in combination with picking
(left) and without (right)

(∩), which is playing a lower note on the same string by forcefully pulling
the higher note off the fretboard to excite a lower note pressed by another
finger. It is easier to excite a string with the pick and then proceed with
a series of hammer-ons and pull-offs, but avoiding picking altogether is also
an option (Figure 6).

Pull-off and hammer-on legato are usually performed by the fretting hand.
However, the picking hand can also play melodic notes by tapping (T) a finger
on the fretboard to extend legato phrases. In metal music, such *tapping* has often
been incorporated to play arpeggios on one string (Figure 7).

These legato techniques can be combined with *slides* (\ or / depending on the
direction). When the finger shifts up or down on the same string without
releasing pressure, such slides produce a fluid, gliding sound (Figure 8).

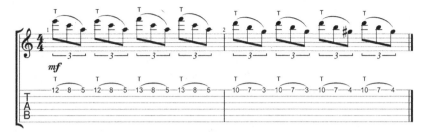

Figure 7 Tapping arpeggios

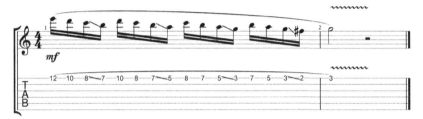

Figure 8 Legato phrase with slides

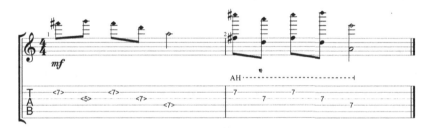

Figure 9 Flageolets (left) and artificial overtones with a fifth interval (right)

Percussive playing techniques include *rakes*, which are grace notes played before articulated notes. Other techniques are adopted from the bass, such as slapping and popping. They have no standardised form of notation, but are sometimes indicated by S and P, respectively. Palm-muting can be a percussive technique if the note's duration is significantly shortened.

Harmonic techniques include flageolets, where a finger is placed on the string without pressing it down on the fretboard to produce a bell-like sound (◇). Flageolets create natural overtones. Artificial overtones (AH) are produced by picking a string with the plectrum while touching it with the picking hand's thumb, resulting in a squealing sound (Figure 9).

The techniques explained here are electric guitar standard techniques that virtuosos have modified over time. This development is outlined in Sections 4 to 6, illustrated by audio and video examples and sheet music where applicable.

4 First-Generation Rock Guitar Heroes

Section 2 gave an overview of canonical electric and rock guitar players as portrayed in guitar handbooks and popular media. In this section, we outline the contributions of electric guitarists that influenced generations of players to come. The period covered stretches from the 1960s to the late 1980s, a time of musical evolution in rock music and its increasing fusion with jazz and classical music. The study of the development of guitar playing (Sections 4 to 6) is based on a combination of discourse tracing from journalistic, practical, and academic sources and musical analysis drawing on our own socialisation and experience in rock guitar scenes.

According to the canonical analysis, Jimi Hendrix is among the most influential electric guitarists today. Building on earlier popular-music guitar heroes such as Robert Johnson, Charley Patton, Huddie William 'Leadbelly' Ledbetter, and Blind Lemon Jefferson (see Bennett & Dawe, 2001; Davis, 2003; Hatch & Millward, 1987; Waksman, 1999), Hendrix inspired generations of guitarists by showcasing what is possible on the instrument. Guitar scholar André Millard (2004a, 2004b) and rock sociologist Deena Weinstein (2013) argue that guitar heroes emerged in the 1960s because of technological progress, the development of the instrument, its amplification, and the resultant performance abilities, which enabled guitarists to compete with singers through dramatic performances. Guitar manufacturers, in particular Gibson and Fender, explored instrument designs and began mass fabrication (Kraft, 2004). Amplifiers and effects pedals afforded new sounds and expanded the tonal spectrum, allowing guitarists to customise their equipment for a unique sound (Millard, 2004c). Hendrix used the latest innovations not purely to enhance his playing via gimmicks; technology also became a fundamental part of his style. He employed amplifier distortion and fuzz pedals, played with controlled feedback, wah-wah, flanging, and octave-shifting pedals, and abused the whammy bar (Whiteley, 1990). Hendrix further intensified these sounds with contemporary studio techniques such as delay and reverb, panning, backwards overdubbing, and phase shifting (Schmidt-Horning, 2004: 118–19). Original playing with emotional expression, the ability to seamlessly switch between lead and rhythm playing, and soulful bendings and vibrato made formerly undesired sounds popular and distinguished him from other guitarists (*Editor Choice*, 2020). In every list of the greatest players of all time that we analysed, Hendrix is declared the most influential guitar hero for his use of effects and for turning distortion and noise into an art form (Kitts & Tolinski, 2002: 25; *Total Guitar*, 2020; *Vintage Guitar*, 2018). While other guitarists also experimented with distorted sounds and some of Hendrix's trademark elements, he made these 'part of a virtuoso's vocabulary of extravagance and transgression', according to metal scholar Robert Walser (1992: 279).

Ritchie Blackmore, Deep Purple's original guitarist, built on Hendrix's virtuosity (Walser, 1992: 268). According to the previously proposed canons, his most significant contribution is his fusion of blues, rock, and classical music, as first heard in 'Demon's Eye' (Deep Purple, 1971)[1] [audio] and 'Highway Star' (Deep Purple, 1972) [audio], with their baroque chord progressions, Bach-like arpeggios, and harmonic minor modes (Kitts & Tolinski, 2002: 42; Thorpe, 2016: 19; Schauss, 2012: 97). Contrary to the common practice of improvising solos, Blackmore composed the melody for 'Highway Star': It 'was well planned . . . I wanted a very definite Bach sound, which is why I wrote it out – and why I played those very rigid arpeggios across that very familiar Bach progression . . . I believe that I was the first person to do that so obviously on the guitar' (Blackmore, in Kitts & Tolinski, 2002: 136). With the popularisation of neoclassical rock and metal, Blackmore opened up new avenues for later players, including Eddie Van Halen, Yngwie Malmsteen, Michael Schenker, and Steve Morse, according to *Guitar World* writers Jeff Kitts and Brad Tolinski (2002: 42). Several writers of guitar handbooks, such as Alexander Reyes (2020), German Schauss (2012), and Rob Thorpe (2016), have similarly described Blackmore as a neoclassical shred pioneer.

For guitarist and educator Joe Stump, the former Scorpions guitarists Uli Jon Roth and Michael Schenker belong to the 'Holy Trinity of European hard rock/ metal guitar' (Stump, 2017: 81). These two German guitarists, along with the British Ritchie Blackmore, experimented with integrating classical elements into rock music. Uli Jon Roth's impact on rock guitar virtuosity is sometimes overlooked (*Guitar World*, 2015). His playing on the Scorpions' albums, starting with *Virgin Killer* (Scorpions, 1976) [audio], provided a template for later neoclassical shredders such as Yngwie Malmsteen, Adrian Vandenberg, and John Norum, according to Kitts and Tolinski (2002: 47). Inspired by Hendrix and Blackmore, Roth experimented with Eastern-sounding Phrygian modes and harmonic minor scales, dramatic tremolo bar phrasing, open string licks, and fast and precise melodic runs, as heard in 'The Sails of Charon' (Scorpions, 1977) [audio], a track Malmsteen covered on his album *Inspiration* (Malmsteen, 1996) [audio]. On the symphonic rock album *Beyond the Astral Skies* (Electric Sun, 1985) [audio], Roth played a seven-string guitar, followed by experiments with imitating the high notes of a violin (Reyes, 2020: 7) with

---

[1] For details on how to access the supplementary audio and video works referenced in this Element, please see the Listening and Media Examples section at the end of the Element.

his Sky Guitars, specially commissioned with thirty to thirty-five frets. According to *Guitar World*, 'Ritchie Blackmore gets most of the credit as a guiding light of the Eighties shred phenomenon notwithstanding that Uli Jon Roth established the blueprint for neoclassical metal through his highly sophisticated guitar playing' (*Guitar World*, 2015).

Another impetus for neoclassical-influenced shred metal guitar came from Randy Rhoads. Soon after his brief engagement in Quiet Riot, he recorded Ozzy Osbourne's two most successful albums, *The Blizzard of Ozz* (Osbourne, 1980a) [audio] and *Diary of a Madman* (Osbourne, 1981b) [audio], before his passing in 1982. As a classically trained guitarist, he brought theory-informed harmonic minor scale runs, diminished arpeggios, and classically influenced melodies into mainstream metal, as can be heard on the baroque-inspired 'Over the Mountain' (Osbourne, 1981c) [audio] or his finger-picked classical piece 'Dee' (Osbourne, 1980b) [audio]. Rhoads used many techniques of the time, such as fast palm-muted picking, legato, and tapping. His double-tapping style of right-finger tapping, left-hand legato, and right-finger tapping, followed by three left-hand legato notes in a sextuplet phrase (Figure 10), was highly influential, not least because of his signature solo on 'Crazy Train' (Osbourne, 1981a) [audio 2:58–3:04] (Govan, 2002a: 59; Thorpe, 2019: 57; Zoupa, 2018: 67). Furthermore, his practice of double-tracking solos with two identical performances, which inspired other notable players such as 'Dimebag' Darrell, is still remembered today, as per Kitts and Tolinski (2002: 129–30, 140).

According to journalist Brad Tolinski (2017: 250–1), Kitts and Tolinski (2002: 49), and guitar manual author Anthony George (2019: 81), Eddie Van Halen is the most influential electric guitar innovator since Jimi Hendrix due to his impact on the many virtuosos who came after him. He was not the first guitarist to play the two-handed tapping legato technique, yet it is his most cited trademark (*Guitar World*, 2015; Rensen & Stösser, 2011: 351; Zoupa, 2018: 66), showcased in 'Eruption' (Van Halen, 1978b) [audio 0:56–1:24, video 1:47–2:10] (Figure 11).

However, Van Halen's influence on electric guitar playing goes far beyond tapping. Manual writer Thorpe (2016: 30–1) and *Rolling Stone* (2015) magazine

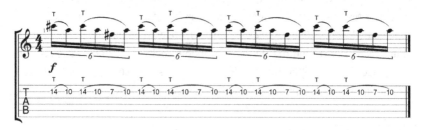

Figure 10. Example of Randy Rhoads' characteristic double tapping style

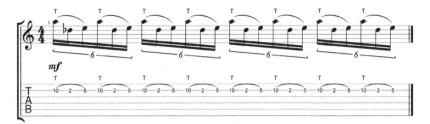

Figure 11 Extract of a tapping sequence in 'Eruption'

regard Van Halen's virtuosic playing as emotional and soulful, preserving the blues tradition inherited from hard rock. Academic George Turner (2015: 81) explains Van Halen's musicality through his artistic use of technique in creating catchy melodies, and the Recording Industry Association of America has awarded the band multiple platinum awards for selling in excess of eighty million records (RIAA, 2021). According to guitar scholar Steve Waksman (2003: 126), Van Halen did not lose his blues roots when he popularised guitar virtuosity that 'displaced the presiding blues-based vocabulary of heavy metal in favor of a much more Eurocentric notion of harmonic and melodic complexity'. 'Eruption' (Van Halen, 1978b) is an example of a composed solo. In the final section, Van Halen showcases two-handed legato tapping, using fingers of the picking hand on the fretboard to complement the fretting hand. The impact of this technique on rock and metal music was significant; both journalists (Kitts & Tolinski, 2002: 49) and academics (Walser, 1992: 276) credit the release with reconfiguring the electric guitar and expanding the capabilities of the instrument. Tapping not only allowed for higher speeds but also made it possible to play larger intervals and other ideas that would otherwise require difficult stretches and position shifts on the fretboard (Zoupa, 2018: 66).

Although guitar journalists (Tolinski, 2017: 250–1) and scholars (Turner, 2015: 79; Walser, 1992: 276) acknowledge Eddie Van Halen as the player who popularised the tapping technique within rock and metal music, many others had used it before him (see Thorpe, 2019; Turner, 2015: 79–88): Roy Smeck on the ukulele, as seen in the film *That Goes Double* (Henabery, 1933) [video 1:26–1:43]; Jimmie Webster on 'Fountain Mist' (Webster, 1959b) [video 0:30–1:20]; Emmett Chapman with his Chapman Stick since 1969; Steve Hackett on 'The Musical Box' (Genesis, 1971) [audio 4:29–4:32, video 4:36–4:40]. By the mid-1970s, fusion guitarists Frank Zappa and Allan Holdsworth and bassist Billy Sheehan also experimented with tapping technique and influenced Eddie Van Halen (Lalaina, 2011; Thorpe, 2016: 111). According to Tolinski (2017: 250–1), Van Halen capitalised on the technique for longer lines played at a fast speed. He also performed phrasings that were usually played with the fretting hand with the tapping finger. For example, he would slide with the tapping hand on the higher frets to produce a more slippery sound. Van Halen also inverted the left and right hand which, besides making for a spectacular show, gave him artificial open strings with pitches other than tuning, adding to the potential of the technique (Govan, 2002a: 64). He used several fingers of his picking hand on the fretboard, known as multi-finger tapping. Again, others practised this technique before him, including Dave Bunker's multi-finger melodic tapping and simultaneous harmonic accompaniment on his Touch Guitar since 1955 [video 0:56–2:26], Jimmy Webster's eight-finger tapping in 'Caravan' (Webster, 1959a) [video 2:30–2:53], and the documented two-finger tapping by Italian amateur guitarist Vittorio Camardese in 1965 (Belladonna, 2013) [video 1:11–1:44]. Van Halen also used 'tapped harmonics': the percussive slap-tapping on the fret-wire five, seven, or twelve frets above the fretted note (Neyens, 2020: 28–9), as heard in 'Spanish Fly' (Van Halen, 1979) [audio 0:00–0:10, video 0:05–0:20] (Figure 12). Such tapped harmonics have a similar timbre to bells, with the attack of a harpsichord.

Van Halen is recognised in the canons primarily due to his ever-evolving playing (Waksman, 2003). Another reason, according to fellow guitarist Zakk Wylde, is his unrelenting search for novel ideas:

> On their first record he did 'Eruption', and people said, what's he gonna do on the next record? So he does 'Spanish Fly'. Then he does 'Cradle Will Rock'. So by the fourth record, you figure, well, he can't beat that. So he fuckin' does 'Mean Streets'! And you go, is that even a *guitar*? What the fuck is he doing? (McIver, 2008: 200)

'Mean Street' (Van Halen, 1981) [audio 0:00–0:23, video 0:00–0:23] features percussive harmonics produced with a tapping technique that mimics the slapping technique of funk bassists (Waksman, 2003: 125–6). In 'Cathedral' (Van Halen, 1982) [audio, video 0:25–1:22], Van Halen emulates a violin by altering the guitar's characteristic envelope shape with the volume control (Govan, 2002a:

Figure 12 Tapped harmonics in 'Spanish Fly'

108). To achieve greater speeds and contrast two opposing sounds of aggression and fluidity, Van Halen generally mixes picking and legato, as heard in the outro of 'I'm the One' (Van Halen, 1978c) [audio 2:44–2:36] (Figure 13).

Guitar manual writer Greg Harrison (2009: 20) calls this technique 'partial picking', and it influenced later players such as 'Dimebag' Darrell. Van Halen's frequent use of the whammy bar can be heard in 'Ain't Talkin'' 'Bout Love' (Van Halen, 1978a) [audio 0:18–0:20, 1:34–1:37, video 1:22–1:35], and his tremolo picking, the rapid repetition of notes, in 'Eruption' (Van Halen, 1978b) [audio 0:30–0:38, video 4:14–4:32] (Figure 14).

The variety of Van Halen's solo techniques should not detract from his contribution to the instrument's technological development (see Waksman, 2004). He invented the 'superstrat' guitar model, popular with many virtuosos since the mid-1980s. Van Halen created this by combining the full-bodied sound of a Les Paul with the easier-to-play Stratocaster model on his self-built Frankenstrat guitar and integrating a Les Paul humbucker pickup into a Stratocaster. He is also credited for his part in introducing the locking tremolo system, inspiring guitarist Floyd Rose to develop the eponymous tremolo system (Tolinski, 2017: 252–3), another feature of the metal guitar and popular with virtuosos. The highly distorted 'brown tone' (Turner & Rubin, 2020) produced by Van Halen's modified Marshall amplifier is characteristic of his sound (Waksman, 2004; Walser, 1992). Due to their capability to produce heavily distorted but

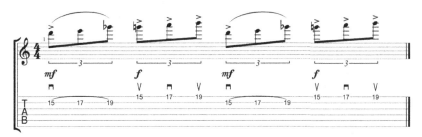

Figure 13 Example of partial picking at the end of the solo of 'I'm the One'

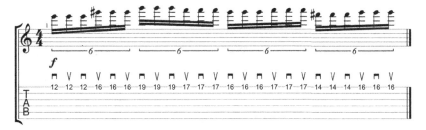

Figure 14 Tremolo picking in the solo of 'Eruption'

transparent tones, his various signature amplifiers from Peavey and Fender remain the foundation of modern metal guitar sounds (Mynett, 2017).

With Joe Satriani and Steve Vai, to whom *Guitar World* (2015) attributes the popularity of the instrumental guitar album in the late 1980s and early 1990s, two guitarists are included in the various greatest lists though they were not the first to release solo guitar albums. Satriani's *Not of this Earth* (Satriani, 1986a) [audio] and especially *Surfing with the Alien* (Satriani, 1987c) [audio] 'took all the rock guitar virtuosity that had gone before . . . and brought it all a giant step further, adding a few new tricks to the lexicon of hot guitar moves and upping the land speed record for notes-per-nanosecond' (*Guitar World*, 2015). Notwithstanding the extravagant display of technique, the quality of compositions, immersive soundscape, groove, and memorable melodies appealed to guitar fans and rock mainstream alike (*Guitar Metrics*, 2019; *Vintage Guitar*, 2018). Satriani's portfolio includes fifteen Grammy Award nominations in the category 'Best Rock Instrumental Performance' (Recording Academy, 2021) and several radio hits. Satriani has taught other canonical guitar players, such as Steve Vai and Kirk Hammett. He is the founder of the annual G3 concert tour, on which two other virtuosos appear alongside him. Additionally, he has several pieces of signature equipment, such as guitars by Ibanez and amplifiers that have changed over the years.

Satriani uses a fluid legato technique equally for speed and ornamentation around melody notes (Brooks, 2018a: 104). His legato lines often stay on one or two strings, allowing smoother and more consistent tones, as can be heard in 'Flying in a Blue Dream' (Satriani, 1989a) [audio 1:36–1:53, video 3:20–3:28]. Satriani popularised tapping with the pick instead of a finger, which produces a brighter and more aggressive sound when played as fast trills (Neyens, 2020: 29–30). He performs it as a trill in his signature song, 'Satch Boogie' (Satriani, 1987b) [audio 1:19–1:24, video 1:04–1:12] (Figure 15). Before him, other players performed tapping with a pick, such as Frank Zappa on 'Black Napkins' (Zappa, 1976) [audio 2:50–2:55, video 2:57–3:04]. Another creative approach in Satriani's playing is evident in 'Midnight' (Satriani, 1987a) [audio,

Figure 15 Pick-tapping for trill effect in the style of 'Satch Boogie'

video], where a combined chord-melody arrangement is realised by extending the fretting hand with two fingers of the picking hand. It also features rhythmic grooves through tapping for chordal stabs (Govan, 2002a: 76).

Steve Vai attracted attention by joining the bands of Frank Zappa, ex-Van Halen's David Lee Roth, and Whitesnake. He made a name for himself as a solo artist with *Flex-Able* (Vai, 1984) [audio] and his acclaimed *Passion and Warfare* (Vai, 1990b) [audio] album. As a distinctive virtuoso, Vai has been continuously featured in guitar media for almost forty years, not least for the practice routines he wrote about in his book *Steve Vai's Guitar Workout* (Vai, 2004). He has a unique style (*Guitar Metrics*, 2019; *Vintage Guitar*, 2018) that can best be described as experimental and transgressive, as exemplified by a *Guitar World* (2015) quote: 'His astounding technique defies categorization. In his graceful hands, the guitar becomes a cosmic antenna, channeling other dimensions and parallel universes'. Guitar media *Guitar Metrics* (2019) and *Vintage Guitar* (2018) see Vai, like Hendrix, as a sound artist who creates music through a coherent blend of playing the instrument and enhancing it with effects.

Vai's daily routine includes practising feel for one hour, which he calls the 'sensitivity hour' (Vai, 2004: 11). Journalists Michael Rensen and Vilim Stösser (2011: 345) describe his expression as 'voice-like'. Next to standard phrasing techniques such as bending and vibrato, Vai frequently uses the wah-wah effect to emulate singing. He utilises the whammy bar – the 'guitar equivalent of a vocalist adding "woahs" and "yeahs" between lines of lyrics' (Thorpe, 2016: 89) – to enhance voice-like expression further through effective pitch and tone modulation. The emotional application of the wah-wah effect is demonstrated in 'Tender Surrender' (Vai, 1995b) [audio 2:48–3:10, video 2:48–3:10], and the whammy bar in 'Bad Horsie' (Vai, 1995a) [audio 0:00–0:23, video 0:00–0:23]. For Rensen and Stösser (2011: 345), imitating the voice with the guitar distinguishes Vai from other neoclassical players who emulate violins and from fusion guitarists taking inspiration from saxophone and horn instruments.

Steve Vai's engagement in instrument design shaped metal guitar playing (see Section 6.1). Instrument modifications like those Eddie Van Halen made to optimise the guitar for his playing style (see Waksman, 2004) encouraged Vai to ask Ibanez, the manufacturer of his signature guitar, for specific alterations: increasing the number of frets from twenty-two to twenty-four; introducing the humbucker, single-coil, humbucker (HSH) pickup configuration; and removing wood under the bridge to allow modulating the pitch up and down with the whammy bar (Tolinski, 2017: 261–2). Vai's signature JEM became the first mass-produced seven-string guitar, the Universe model, which nu and industrial metal bands such as Korn and Fear Factory embraced in the 1990s to modernise the sound of metal (Gil, 2014).

The first-generation rock guitar virtuosos pushed the boundaries beyond what was believed possible or aesthetically accepted. Standard techniques were developed further in the pursuit of individual styles. The limitations of standard instruments and amplification technologies prompted guitarists either to make modifications themselves or to convince manufacturers to develop them. Their persistence contributed to advancements in guitar technology (see Herbst, 2016). The continuous development of the instrument enabled guitarists to realise their creative visions. It also resulted in commodified products, helping later players in their search for new means of expression. According to popular discourse, as analysed through guitar-specific media, few of the discussed guitarists performed virtuosity solely for the sake of technique. Relevant to mainstream success was the quality of their musical compositions, something that fewer of the later players achieved.

5 The Emergence and Decline of Shred

Virtuosos playing in hair metal bands and making a name for themselves as solo artists had their heydays in the 1980s and early 1990s. Not all guitarists were classically oriented and could be subsumed under the neoclassical label, so the term 'shred' appeared and became synonymous with the virtuoso rock guitar genre (Waksman, 2003: 127). This section explores the rise of shred facilitated by Shrapnel Records, followed by discussing advances in playing, performance, and technology between the mid-1980s and the early 2000s.

5.1 Shrapnel Records and The Rise of Shred

Shrapnel Records has been a significant label in the popularisation of virtuosic electric guitar playing. Mike Varney founded it in 1980 as a record company dedicated exclusively to metal music, preceding better-known metal labels such as Metal Blade (1982), Megaforce (1982), Music For Nations (1983), Nuclear Blast (1987), and Century Media (1988). When metal was booming and new bands continually emerging, Shrapnel founder and guitar enthusiast Varney decided to specialise in instrumental guitar-focused music to distinguish his label from mainstream metal. Varney's primary motivation was to help the US guitar scene catch up with the developments in Europe: 'In Europe there were all these great guitarists, from Eric Clapton and Uli Jon Roth to Jeff Beck and Michael Schenker. In the States we had one major guitar hero in Jimi Hendrix and then, later, Eddie Van Halen. My initial goal was to find the next great guitar hero in the US' (Lalaina, 2008: 72). With metal music becoming popular in the USA, Varney contributed his 'Spotlight' column to *Guitar Player* magazine, which he used to raise the profiles of promising rock guitar virtuosos.

The popularity of the column encouraged numerous guitarists to send him demo tapes. According to journalist Joe Lalaina, at a 'time when virtuoso guitar playing was coming to the fore, Varney was the *American Idol* for the chops-intensive guitar sect' (Lalaina, 2008: 70). Varney stated that he selected one guitarist for a record out of every 1,000 tapes received (Lalaina, 2008: 70). Among the players featured in Spotlight were Yngwie Malmsteen, Paul Gilbert, Vinnie Moore, Shawn Lane, and Scott Henderson.

Yngwie Malmsteen sent a demo tape to Varney in 1983. Malmsteen was inspired by violinist Niccolò Paganini and also studied the neoclassical styles of Ritchie Blackmore, Uli Jon Roth, and Randy Rhoads. Taking classically influenced rock and metal music one step further made him a role model for numerous shredders, and for Shrapnel's catalogue (Walser, 1992: 299). Malmsteen's first notable appearance was on the self-titled debut album of US hair metal band Steeler (Steeler, 1983) [audio]. As one of Shrapnel's best-selling releases, the album 'gave encouragement to the other high-level guitarists out there who'd been sitting in their bedrooms practicing all these years', in Varney's words (Lalaina, 2008: 72). Malmsteen's debut solo album, *Rising Force* (Malmsteen, 1984c) [audio], released not by Shrapnel but by Polydor, was perceived as impactful in the rock guitar world as Van Halen's debut, according to several journalistic sources (*Guitar World*, 2015; Kitts & Tolinski, 2002: 45). Critics said Malmsteen's compositions were a mere amalgamation of his icons of baroque and classical music in a more modern metal sound (Heritage, 2016; Walser, 1992), but the popular hybrid realised with 'unapologetic fury' (Brooks, 2017: 5) and advanced playing skills nonetheless set a 'new standard for speed, grace and virtuosity' (Kitts & Tolinski, 2002: 45) in the post-Van Halen era and 'inspired an era of innovation and accelerated evolution in the world of guitar' (Reyes, 2020: 5).

Malmsteen's neoclassical, violin-inspired sound features well-known musical elements: extended single-string melodies, positional and shifting scale patterns, tonal sequencing, pedal-point licks and Bach-like inverted pedal-point melodies, diminished arpeggios, the Phrygian dominant mode, harmonisation in third intervals, violin vibrato, and regular use of the volume potentiometer for violin-like swells (Brooks, 2017). The opening track of Malmsteen's solo debut, 'Black Star' (Malmsteen, 1984a) [audio 0:50–1:02], is frequently cited in guitar discourse as an example of his style (*Guitar Metrics*, 2019; Thorpe, 2016: 19; Walser, 1992: 293–4). Noteworthy is Malmsteen's unconventional way of picking the strings. Instead of alternating downstrokes and upstrokes, his picking changes depending on whether the lines are ascending or descending, based on a complex set of considerations that includes string-changing strategies, scale layout, and melodic choices (Brooks, 2017: 36). Malmsteen uses economy

Figure 16 Example of Malmsteen's pick-gato

picking for ascending scale runs while picking descending lines with three notes per string with alternate picking. This approach can improve speed because the pick glides smoothly from one string to the next (Brooks, 2017: 56). Another of Malmsteen's approaches is 'pick-gato', where large movements of the picking hand are avoided when exercising alternate picking. Moreover, this uses the advantages of alternate picking to start picking strings with downstrokes and strategically employs legato to prevent altering the pick orientation when changing strings (Brooks, 2017: 59) (Figure 16).

The sweep picking technique in metal music is associated with Malmsteen, according to journalists Brad Tolinski (2017: 251–2), Chris Brooks (2017: 5), *Guitar World* (2015), and academic Robert Walser (1992: 293–4), much like tapping is associated with Eddie Van Halen (Thorpe, 2019: 78). However, guitarists utilised sweeping before him, such as Django Reinhardt, Chet Atkins, Ritchie Blackmore, and Jan Akkerman. Malmsteen popularised the most common arpeggio pattern across three and five strings through early songs like 'Far Beyond the Sun' (Malmsteen, 1984b) [audio 4:47–4:50, video 5:06–5:14]. He built more songs on sweep-picked arpeggios on later releases such as 'Demon Driver' (Malmsteen, 1990) [audio 1:35–1:55] and 'Blitzkrieg' (Malmsteen, 1999) [audio 1:06–1:17].

According to Malmsteen scholar Brooks (2017: 63–4), another of Malmsteen's trademark techniques is his floating between rhythmic subdivisions, which creates a rushing effect and the illusion of higher speeds than performed (Brooks, 2017: 102, 155; Thorpe, 2016: 97). Guitar educator Herman (2014: 15) claims this illusion arises from Malmsteen's clean picking with clear note definition.

Unlike many of Malmsteen's later records, *Rising Force* (Malmsteen, 1984c) [audio] was an instrumental album that inspired a wave of instrumental guitar albums by 'hyper-virtuosic players' (Walser, 1992: 299) in the 1980s, many of which were released by Shrapnel. Varney did not downplay Malmsteen's influence, but also emphasised that the 'shred guitar scene was formed by the culmination of a bunch of guitarists collectively' (Lalaina, 2008: 72). After

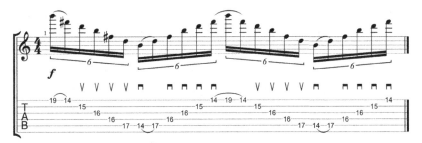

Figure 17 Sweep-picked arpeggio in 'Altitudes'

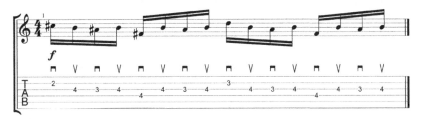

Figure 18 Internal pedal in 'Race with Destiny'

releasing *Steeler* (Steeler, 1983), Shrapnel brought out the first albums by shredders who entered the canons of virtuosos or electric guitarists (see Section 2): Tony MacAlpine with *Edge of Insanity* (MacAlpine, 1985a) [audio]; Paul Gilbert with *Street Lethal* (Racer X, 1986) [audio] and *Second Heat* (Racer X, 1987b) [audio]; Vinnie Moore with *Mind's Eye* (Moore, 1986) [audio]; Jason Becker and Marty Friedman with *Speed Metal Symphony* (Cacophony, 1987) [audio], *Perpetual Burn* (Becker, 1988b) [audio], and *Dragon's Kiss* (Friedman, 1988) [audio]; Greg Howe with *Greg Howe* (Howe, 1988) [audio]; and Richie Kotzen with *Richie Kotzen* (Kotzen, 1989) [audio]. Compilation albums featured other known virtuosos, such as Michael Angelo Batio and Shawn Lane. They all used neoclassical techniques, as popularised by Malmsteen, and developed them further. For example, Jason Becker made regular use of extensive five- and six-string sweep-picked arpeggios, best represented in 'Altitudes' (Becker, 1988a) [audio 1:58–2:24] (Figure 17). Vinnie Moore frequently played pedal-note melodies, as in 'Race with Destiny' (Moore, 1988) [audio 0:20–0:34], where one or more notes are repeated in a motif (Figure 18). Tony MacAlpine relied on the Phrygian dominant scale, the fifth mode of the harmonic minor scale. An example is 'Wheel of Fortune' (MacAlpine, 1985b) [audio].

Shrapnel boss Varney produced and engineered all albums (Wiederhorn, 2015), giving them a recognisable sonic signature. Handling everything from signing to producing artists had financial motivations. According to Varney, the total cost for most albums was under $1,000, including artwork, because it took less than 100 hours to record and mix them (Wiederhorn, 2015). Roles were sometimes shared, and Shrapnel artists produced records by fellow guitarists (Wiederhorn, 2015). Shrapnel records thus had a relatively poor sound quality compared to the mainstream metal releases of the time, many of which were engineered and produced by professionals such as Michael Wagener, Flemming Rasmussen, and Andy Wallace. In contrast to Shrapnel's low outlays, Wagener stated in an interview that his usual budgets for rock production in the 1980s were between $250,000 and $500,000 (Leibundgut, 2000).

Shrapnel artists toured less frequently than traditional rock and metal bands due to Varney's label philosophy: 'A lot of those guys didn't do a lot of touring on their own. Labels who were interested would say, "I want to see the band live," and I'd tell them, "I don't care." I never saw myself being anything other than a producer. More of a producer than a label' (Wiederhorn, 2015). Virtuoso Marty Friedman confirmed that Shrapnel artists were not promoted at all: there were no magazine advertisements, videos, or tours (Wiederhorn, 2015). Making a living solely from their music was near impossible, so many of Shrapnel's guitarists had extra jobs, such as factory work or teaching guitar. One way around the need for a regular job was to join more commercial bands with singers (Wiederhorn, 2015): Paul Gilbert founded Mr. Big in 1988; Marty Friedman joined Megadeth in 1990; Richie Kotzen became a member of Poison in 1991 and Mr. Big in 1999; and Jason Becker joined as the guitarist of David Lee Roth's solo band in 1991. Instructional videos provided another source of income, and had a profound impact on the scene. Many Shrapnel guitarists and other virtuosos made instructional videos for companies such as REH, Alfred, Hal Leonard, Young Guitar, and the Metal Method (Table 6).

Such videos by rock guitar virtuosos, providing structured instruction and technical exercises (Lalaina, 2008: 72), changed learning significantly. Aspiring guitarists now had an alternative to copying records by ear. With shredders revealing their playing secrets in their videos, a general surge in speed and dexterity followed. Rock journalist Wiederhorn sees such videos as a major reason why by the 'end of the 80s, the scene had turned into an absurd musical arms race to see who could be the fastest player around' (Wiederhorn, 2015). Altogether, the lack of touring and promotion made the music and instructional videos by Shrapnel artists one of the scene's main communication channels between the virtuosos and the 'legions of semi-professional and would-be metal guitarists' (Walser, 1992: 299) in an era before Web 2.0. They prepared the scene for later online video and social media developments.

Table 6 Shred guitar instructional videos in the late 1980s to mid-1990s

Guitarist	Video	Publisher
Becker, Jason	Jason Becker (1989) [information, video]	Hal Leonard
Bouillet, Bruce	Improvisation for Progressive Hard Rock Guitar (1989) [video]	Silver Eagle
Friedman, Marty	Melodic Control (1993) [video]	Inside Edge Productions / Alfred
	The Essential (1996) [video]	Rittor Music
Gilbert, Paul	Intense Rock 1 (1988) [video]	REH
	Intense Rock 2 (1991) [video]	REH
	Terrifying Guitar Trip (1995) [video]	REH
	Guitars from Mars 1 (1996) [video]	Young Guitar
	Guitars from Mars 2 (1996) [video]	Young Guitar
Howe, Greg	Hot Rock Licks (1992) [video]	REH
Johnson, Eric	Total Electric Guitar (1990) [information]	Hal Leonard
Kotzen, Richie	Rock Chops (1989) [video]	REH
Lane, Shawn	Power Solos (1993) [video]	REH
	Power Licks (1995) [video]	REH
Lynch, George	Guitar Bible (1989) [video]	Sacred Groove Records
	George Lynch (1990) [video]	REH
MacAlpine, Tony	Tony MacAlpine (1990) [video]	REH
	Shred Guitar (1992) [video]	REH
Malmsteen, Yngwie	Yngwie Malmsteen (1991) [video]	REH
	Play Loud 1 & 2 (1995) [video, video]	Young Guitar
Moore, Vinnie	Speed, Accuracy and Articulation (1989) [video]	REH
	Advanced Lead Guitar Techniques (1990) [video]	REH
Petrucci, John	Rock Discipline (1995) [video]	REH
Satriani, Joe	The Satch Tapes (1992) [video]	Relativity
Vai, Steve	Steve Vai: Styles & Secrets (1995) [information]	Omnibus

Shrapnel's artists were academically acknowledged for their avant-garde achievements that valued originality and technique (Walser, 1992: 299). Guitar scholars also noticed them being accused 'of the sins of virtuosity levied against Liszt and Chopin – talented purveyors (or victims) of self-indulgent, vacuous expression' (Fellezs, 2018: 117) and 'undesirable foregrounding of musical technique' (Waksman, 2003: 126). Neoclassical shred has not disappeared, to which canonical players who have continued this style give evidence, such as Symphony X's Michael Romeo, Children of Bodom's Alexi Laiho, and Nevermore's Jeff Loomis.

5.2 Developments in Playing by Canonical Rock Guitarists

Few of the playing techniques used by virtuosos in the 1980s and 1990s were entirely new; however, the virtuosos took them to new speeds and combined playing styles in various ways characteristic of compositions of the shred genre. An emphasis on technical ability distinguished shred guitarists from former rock virtuosos. How established techniques were modified and advanced is addressed next.

Alternate picking was one of the standard techniques taken to a new pace; 1980s virtuosos such as Vinnie Moore, Greg Howe, and Paul Gilbert explored this technique, drawing on fusion guitarists like John McLaughlin and Al Di Meola. According to guitar manual author Chris Basener (2011: 12), Gilbert took up the trick of 1970s guitarists of repeating short pentatonic phrases to build excitement, which earned him a reputation for fast repeated scalar licks with three notes per string. These notes he played at a constant tempo or accelerated for an exaggerated dramatic effect, as in 'Viking Kong' (Racer X, 2000) [audio 2:49–3:26, video 3:36–4:15]. The picked and legato notes are combined to produce a fast and aggressive sound, thus demonstrating Gilbert's version of Malmsteen's pick-gato approach (Figure 19).

Gilbert relied on the ergonomic benefits of scalar runs played with three-note-per-string patterns, rather than the classical box position with a mixture of two and three notes per string, like most other Shrapnel artists (Alexander, 2018: 33)

Figure 19 Combination of alternate picking and legato in 'Viking Kong'

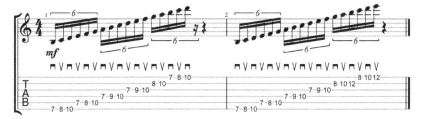

Figure 20 Box scale (left) with an irregular number of notes per string and a three-note-per-string scale (right)

(Figure 20). This may seem a minor difference, yet alternate picking becomes easier and maximum speed can be increased due to the symmetric nature of three-note-per-string scales.

Racer X's 'Scarified' (Racer X, 1987a) [audio, video] contains such three-note-per-string runs in both the main riff (Figure 21) and the twin guitar solo by Paul Gilbert and Bruce Bouillet. This solo style, with three-note-per-string sextuplet runs and patterns based on Randy Rhoads' style, is still most strongly associated with Shrapnel and 1980s shredding, according to handbook author Joseph Alexander (2018: 33). The popularity of three-note-per-string scales can be explained by the beneficial ergonomics of symmetric picking and fretting (see Section 3), which is why guitar educator Joe Stump (2014: 2) has labelled them 'speed scales'. From a contemporary perspective, Alexander (2018: 65) attributes a slightly dated sound to them.

Economy picking was another technique popular in late-1980s rock music. Jazz guitarists already used this technique (Brooks, 2017: 57), as did Yngwie Malmsteen, but only for ascending scale runs (Brooks, 2017: 36, 56). A considerable number of manual writers (Brooks, 2018b: 7; George, 2019: 35, 43, 2020: 25, 155; Govan, 2002a: 42; Harrison, 2009: 37; Thorpe, 2016: 49) agree that fusion guitarist Frank Gambale popularised economy picking with his educational video *Monster Licks & Speed Picking* (Gambale, 1992) [video] (*Total Guitar*, 2020). Economy picking enabled faster playing because the challenges of changing strings with alternate picking, like large motions or being trapped between strings (see Section 3), were eliminated, which is why Gambale called the technique 'speed picking'. Gambale used the technique for arpeggios and runs both up and down the strings, which was different to Malmsteen. This playing style is featured in 'New Boots' (Gambale, 1990) [audio] on the album *Truth in Shredding* [audio]. Fast and clean playing became Gambale's hallmark and influenced virtuosos of various genres (George, 2020: 25), including metal lead guitarists such as Marty Friedman. According to manual writer Rob Thorpe (2016: 49), Friedman stood out in metal music of

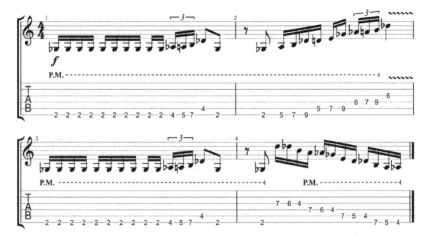

Figure 21 Main motif in 'Scarified' using three-note-per-string runs

the 1980s and 1990s because his economy picking allowed him to break with the scalar melodies that were common at the time due to the prevalence of alternate picking.

Sweeping existed long before Malmsteen and later Shrapnel artists such as Jason Becker and Tony MacAlpine popularised it. Like economy picking, sweeping was already used by jazz artists. An example is Django Reinhardt's 'Improvisation' (Reinhardt, 1935 [2016]) [audio 0:17–0:21], where he applied the technique to ascend three-string arpeggios on a nylon-string guitar. Other early sweep-pickers on the electric guitar were Chet Atkins and Ritchie Blackmore in the 1960s, and Jan Akkerman of Focus in the 1970s, as seen in live performances of Deep Purple's 'Wring That Neck' in 1969 (Jewlampijs95, 2007) [video 1:41–1:55)] and Focus' 'Hocus Pocus' in 1973 (Jackson, 2007) [video 2:53–2:55]. Virtuosos from the 1980s onwards built entire phrases and sections on sweeping technique. Compared to the 1980s standard, both Akkerman's and Blackmore's occasional sweeping of single arpeggios seem rather messy and lacking in proper technique. Shred guitarists developed different ways of muting unused strings with both hands when sweeping to control noise and ringing notes (see Vallejo, 2020: 22–4). They also created more variation by combining sweeping with other techniques, such as fretting-hand legato and tapping, for longer phrases and higher speed. MacAlpine, for example, tended to add a tapped note towards the end of his sweeping passages, as in 'Hundreds of Thousands' (MacAlpine, 1987) [audio 0:41–0:42, see also video] (Figure 22).

Even more characteristic is that MacAlpine did not always use his plectrum to sweep arpeggios, but instead played one-note-per-string hammer-on legato

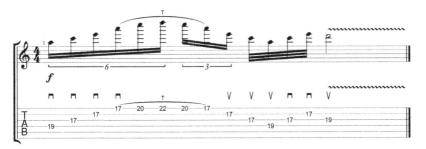

Figure 22 Sweep-tapping in 'Hundreds of Thousands'

[video]. Joe Satriani used this technique for larger intervals, as heard on 'The Mystical Potato Head Groove Thing' (Satriani, 1989b) [audio 1:31–1:42, video 1:31–1:44]. Brett Garsed, Eric Johnson, and Zakk Wylde explored another alternative to playing one-note-per-string phrases: country-inspired 'chicken picking', using a combination of pick and fingers, as in 'Devil's Daughter' (Osbourne, 1988) [audio 3:28–3:34, video 0:16–0:22]. According to educator Greg Harrison (2009: 61), this is not only fast, but strings can also be skipped, breaking up scalar melodies even more than sweeping does. Steve Morse, Paul Gilbert, Marty Friedman, John Petrucci, and Michael Romeo were among the players who preferred alternate or economy picking to play larger intervals and arpeggios by skipping strings. One example of this practice is John Petrucci's solo in 'Erotomania' (Dream Theater, 1994b) [audio 5:08–5:24, video 5:08–5:25] (Figure 23) using string-skipped alternate picking.

String skipping was cultivated in the late 1980s and 1990s to display virtuosity. Manual author George (2020: 89) describes it as a 'highly revered and much-feared technique by many players who see it as extremely advanced'. For other handbook authors such as Harrison (2009: 41), Thorpe (2016: 23), and Zoupa (2018: 39), and virtuoso Govan (2002a: 82), string skipping is a more musical alternative to sweeping. In the outro solo of Guthrie Govan's 'Wonderful Slippery Thing' (Govan, 2006c) [audio 1:22–1:27, video 1:22–1:27] (Figure 24), arpeggios were played with string skipping using one-handed legato or two-handed tapping to avoid the sound of long sweep-picked phrases.

According to educator Zoupa (2018: 111), sweeping was overused in the 1980s. Finding alternatives was thus a step towards more modern solo techniques that tend to rely on advanced legato techniques (see Section 6.2). To this day, however, guitar educators describe the 'ability to execute sweep picked arpeggios [as] represent[ing] the threshold between being an average guitarist or an accomplished guitarist' (Herman, 2014: 88) and as having a 'reputation

Figure 23 Picking string-skipping in 'Erotomania'

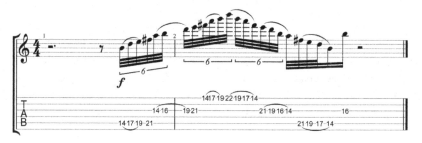

Figure 24 Legato string-skipping in 'Wonderful Slippery Thing'

amongst guitarists as being a terrifying and super-advanced technique that only the best guitarists can master' (George, 2020: 107).

Legato technique was popular with virtuosos because it afforded higher speeds by eliminating the need to synchronise both hands. According to journalists (*Guitar World*, 2015) and educators (Thorpe, 2019: 78), one of the players most influential for later rock guitar virtuosos was 1970s fusion guitarist Allan Holdsworth, who disliked the sound of pull-off legato and therefore used ascending and descending hammer-ons to replicate the evenness of jazz horns and produce a more consistent tone (Brooks, 2018a: 15). Without the help of a tapping finger, he played four notes per string so as not to have to stay in the same fretboard position (*Total Guitar*, 2020). This approach differed from the three-note-per-string runs of Shrapnel artists and the pentatonic boxes popular in the 1960s and 1970s (Figure 25).

Holdsworth's legato technique can be heard in 'The Sixteen Men of Tain' (Holdsworth, 2000) [audio, video]. His style influenced Eddie Van Halen (Kitts & Tolinski, 2002: 44) and newer generations of virtuosos (*Guitar World*, 2015; Thorpe, 2019: 78). Another notable legato player is Greg Howe. He developed Holdsworth's legato approach further (George, 2020: 71) by combining it with palm-muted pull-offs, tapping sequences, and scalar runs involving tapping technique (*Total Guitar*, 2020), as heard on Howe's and Richie Kotzen's collaborative album *Project* (Kotzen & Howe, 1997) [audio]. The technique

Figure 25 Pentatonic box (left), three-note-per-string scale (middle), four-note-per-string scale (right)

of avoiding the picking hand or using it as an equaliser for tonal control by applying different amounts of palm-muting to vary tonal quality was a creative application of legato, whose potential extends into contemporary playing (see Section 6).

Analysing why the players of the 1980s to 2000s discussed here entered the canons suggests the reason to be their influence on later generations of players, just as they had themselves built on the achievements of earlier rock guitar heroes. The difference is that the first generation was influential for several trademarks: playing, technological innovation, and showmanship. In contrast, many shred guitarists became known for one or just a few characteristics, such as mastery of a particular playing technique, as described earlier.

The fact that shredders have received criticism (Fellezs, 2018; Waksman, 2003; Walser, 1992) has not precluded their inclusion in the canons. Several were valued for their emotional playing in the continuing tradition of earlier heroes such as Hendrix and Van Halen, as the analysed greatest lists (see Section 2) suggest. Virtuosos retaining some of the blues elements of former hard rock were generally more palatable, as this balanced the display of technique and placed them more in the middle of the 'technique versus emotion' (Waksman, 2003: 128) debate of the 1990s. A statement by manual author Thorpe is representative of the reasoning behind the appreciation of the blues:

> Blues is a very expressive form of music. Central to this, is the way pitches are manipulated by bending and vibrato to create a vocal delivery, so it is worth noting that the most successful metal guitarists include plenty of blues phrasing in their playing. Metal solos can become overly technical and lose this sense of expression, so tempering the shredding with some blues is a great way to balance the adrenaline and excitement with more emotive ideas. (Thorpe, 2019: 7)

Amongst the players commended for their blues feel are 'Dimebag' Darrell (Thorpe, 2019: 7; *Total Guitar*, 2020), Paul Gilbert (Thorpe, 2019: 5, 20), Kirk Hammett (McIver, 2008: 153–4; Thorpe, 2019: 20; Zoupa, 2018: 50), Richie

Kotzen (George, 2019: 12), George Lynch (Stetina, 1990: 13), and Zakk Wylde (Rensen & Stösser, 2011: 372; Thorpe, 2019: 5). A representative quote highlighting Gilbert's playing style states, 'perfect balance of bluesy expression and vibrato, along with his searing speed [that] helped him rise to fame in the late '80s' (Thorpe, 2019: 20). Gilbert's blues influence is apparent on his solo releases, most notably on his album *Raw Blues Power* (Gilbert & Kid, 2002) [audio]. Such blues influences helped shredders not to be perceived as being overly technical for the sake of technicality (Thorpe, 2019: 7). Musicality is occasionally valued by greatest lists authors (McIver, 2008: 89–91; Rensen & Stösser, 2011: 102, 246; *Guitar Metrics*, 2019) and guitar handbook writers (Govan, 2002b: 11). For example, *Guitar Metrics* (2019) acknowledge John Petrucci for his expressive melodies whilst performing with great speed and accuracy. An example of Petrucci's technical playing for dramatic emotional effect is his solo on 'Voices' (Dream Theater, 1994c) [audio 7:23–8:20, video 7:21–8:19].

Conversely, clean technique and pure speed earned some players recognition in the shred community. The canons repeatedly highlight three guitarists (see Section 2): Rusty Cooley, Michael Angelo Batio, and Shawn Lane. Rusty Cooley is included in the analysed canon of guitar manuals merely due to his technique. In the 2000s, he was considered the 'fastest shredder on the planet', as per Zoupa (2018: 41). Instructional videos *Shred Guitar Manifesto* (Cooley, 2000) [video] and *Extreme Pentatonics* (Cooley, 2001) [video] made Cooley known before he released his self-titled debut album (Cooley, 2002a) [audio]. Like Cooley, Michael Angelo Batio is better known for his instructional video series *Speed Kills* (Batio, 2003, 2004) [video] than for his neoclassical shred-style music, as featured on his debut album *No Boundaries* (Batio, 1994) [audio]. He has frequently performed as a shred metal spectacle (see also Millard, 2004b) at music conventions such as NAMM, and he developed instrument technology such as the Sawtooth Double Guitar and ChromaCast Signature String Dampener (*Sawtooth World*, 2020). Fusion player Shawn Lane combined advanced technique with a sense of melody and rhythm, which appealed to aspiring guitarists and fellow virtuosos alike, according to *Guitar World* (2015). This playing style can be heard on his second (and final) solo album, *The Tri-Tone Fascination* (Lane, 2000) [audio].

The canons include the criterion of stylistic versatility, distinguishing guitar virtuosos from mere shredders (see Section 2). Among the most accomplished players according to the analysed media are Steve Lukather (Rensen & Stösser, 2011: 181), the Toto guitarist and LA-based session musician with more than a thousand album credits; Steve Morse, of hard rock veterans Deep Purple and jazz-rock band Dixie Dregs (Rensen & Stösser, 2011: 219); and Guthrie Govan

(Bienstock, 2019c). Eric Johnson is comparatively under-represented in the canons (see Section 2). Still, journalists Kitts and Tolinski (2002: 44–5) present him as an example of an all-rounder with an identifiable sound and technique, as demonstrated in his signature song 'Cliffs of Dover' (Johnson, 1990) [audio]. Willingness to experiment is a further necessary criterion. For example, several guitar magazines value John McLaughlin as a fusion rock player participating in the Mahavishnu Orchestra (*Guitar World*, 2015; *Louder*, 2018; *Rolling Stone*, 2015). Another example is the eccentric guitarist Buckethead, whose 'playing can shift in a 32nd-note triplet from downright weird computer meltdown noises to hauntingly beautiful arpeggios' (*Guitar World*, 2015), as can be heard in 'Sanctum' (Buckethead, 1998) [audio]. *Total Guitar* (2020) called Buckethead one of the guitar's 'last true innovators'.

Harmony and theory are also highlighted in the discourse. For reasons similar to those previously explained for the blues, George (2019: 3) and Thorpe (2019: 7) find that basic pentatonic and blues scales preserve the tradition of earlier, blues-influenced hard rock as well as balancing speed and emotion. Creativity in shred is evident in employing the traditional scale in novel ways. For Thorpe (2019: 7), the pentatonic scale is the opposite of neoclassical shred because of its almost ideological value, which is supported by a *Guitar World* quote about 'Dimebag' Darrell: 'Dimebag grabbed the baton from players like Eddie Van Halen and Randy Rhoads and proceeded to shove it up the ass of pretentious neoclassical guitarists with his incredibly heavy, unapologetically raw pentatonic shredding' (*Guitar World*, 2015). Manual authors Thorpe (2016: 57, 122; 2019: 7, 20, 106), Zoupa (2018: 50), and George (2019, 2020) point out the creative use of pentatonic scales by Zakk Wylde, 'Dimebag' Darrell, Kirk Hammett, and Paul Gilbert, other than neoclassical idioms based on harmonic minor modes. Wylde's '1,000,000 Miles Away' (Wylde, 1996) [audio 3:57–4:22] shows how pentatonic runs in Randy Rhoads' tradition still work in a more contemporary context.

The academisation of guitar virtuosity in the late 1980s and 1990s is also highlighted in popular guitar discourse, for example, regarding harmony through the use of modes. Joe Satriani and Steve Vai are most often cited for using them (Dillard, 2007: 35; George, 2020: 86; Riley, 2004: 42; Thorpe, 2016: 61), especially the Lydian mode, as heard in 'Flying in a Blue Dream' (Satriani, 1989a) [audio]. In the metal context, George (2020), Govan (2002a), and Thorpe (2016) emphasise the use of chromaticism and symmetrical scales, particularly referencing 'Dimebag' Darrell, John Petrucci, and Michael Romeo. Romeo's solo on 'Of Sins and Shadows' (Symphony X, 1997) [audio 3:03–3:13] is an example. Odd time signatures and groupings have likewise been emphasised as characteristic features of players such as Guthrie Govan

(George, 2020: 48, 147), John Petrucci (Riley, 2004: 27; George, 2020: 147), Michael Romeo (Riley, 2004: 25; Thorpe, 2016: 106), and Shawn Lane (Govan 2002a: 27; George, 2020: 147). An example is 'Hangover' (Govan, 2006a) [audio] with groupings of nine. In comparison, groove is less discussed. Alexander (2018: 44–45) and Rensen and Stösser (2011: 33) highlight Nuno Bettencourt as a virtuosic player and master of alternate rhythm and lead playing in Hendrix's tradition: fast playing infused with funk-influenced rhythmic motifs, as in 'Get the Funk Out' (Extreme, 1990) [audio]. Likewise, *Guitar Metrics* (2020) recognises 'Dimebag' Darrell's contribution to Pantera's groove metal style. As with Bettencourt, Darrell's sense of groove goes beyond rhythm playing and forms a crucial part of his soloing style, according to educators (Alexander, 2018: 44) and journalists (*Guitar Metrics*, 2020; *Total Guitar*, 2020).

Shredders received attention for pushing the limits of speed, accuracy, and difficulty. Imitating different instruments was an effective way, too, as the analysed guitar manuals suggest. In contrast to shredders being mere guitarists, virtuosos striving for new expressive forms considered themselves 'musicians who play guitar', according to Govan (2002a: 9). As Holdsworth once stated: 'It's not so much what makes a great guitarist as what makes a great musician, because a guitar is just an instrument, and an instrument is just a tool. A great musician is someone who sticks out like a sore thumb – in a great way' (Kitts & Tolinski, 2002: 116). Govan (2002a: 9) and Thorpe (2016: 123) argue that the guitar always sounds like a guitar, but a player copying other instruments' attributes will develop and may thus become distinct. Fusion players such as Holdsworth, Gambale, and Govan reconfigured the guitar by adopting melodic ideas and phrasing from horn instruments. Govan also explored arpeggios by tapping notes on adjacent strings with his picking hand to adapt his runs to a saxophone sound (George, 2020: 115), as in his song 'Sevens' (Govan, 2006b) [audio 1:08–1:34, video 1:43–2:16] (Figure 26).

Even extreme metal players such as Paul Masvidal of Cynic and Fredrik Thordendal of Meshuggah were inspired by saxophonists like John Coltrane

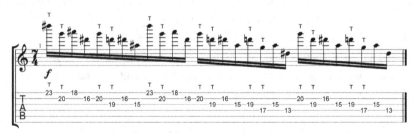

Figure 26 Tapped arpeggios in 'Seven'

and Michael Brecker playing legato (Thorpe, 2016: 123). Yngwie Malmsteen developed his style by mimicking the violin (George, 2020: 19; Govan, 2002a: 104). Danny Gatton and Robben Ford have emulated the Hammond organ, as heard in 'Muthaship' (Gatton, 1991) [audio] (Govan, 2002a: 104), and John 5 imitated the banjo and pedal steel in songs like 'Fiddlers' (John 5, 2005) [audio] (Thorpe, 2016: 123). Buckethead adopted slap-bass techniques in 'Robot Transmission' (Buckethead, 1996) [audio] (Govan, 2002a: 104), and Joe Satriani emulated the mellotron in 'The Snake' (Satriani, 1986b) [audio] (Govan, 2002a: 108). Jazz guitarist Stanley Jordan imitated the piano by extending his fretting hand with multi-finger tapping and extensive use of hammer-on legato (Neyens, 2020: 71, 78), as heard in his arrangement of 'Stairway to Heaven' (Jordan, 1988) [audio, video]. Marty Friedman's music features Japanese koto-influenced curl bendings, pre-bendings, bendings from non-scale tones, and Eastern pentatonic scales that 'make Friedman's style so distinctive' (Govan, 2002b: 12). He has dedicated whole albums to his Japanese inspirations, such as *Tokyo Jukebox* (Friedman, 2009) [audio]; an older example is 'Tibet' (Friedman, 1992) [audio].

Showmanship has rarely been addressed in guitar manuals and greatest lists, though it has been discussed in the scholarly discourse and is relevant in the context of rock guitar virtuosity.

> The focus of the guitarist's performance is a display of intense emotionality, alternating with looks of exertion and concentration. The repertoire of expressions and gestures has by now become ritualized and mannered, understood, although not necessarily on a conscious level, by the audience. Shows of exertion and concentration indicate that the playing is difficult. Looks underscore the virtuosity, which is the antithesis of routine. (Weinstein, 2013: 145)

Nevertheless, most guitar virtuosos stand out for showcasing ease in their playing rather than concentration and effort. Steve Vai makes the most difficult passages look easy, as shown in the DVD *Alien Love Secrets* (Vai, 1998). Likewise, Paul Gilbert's video on 'Technical Difficulties' [audio] from his instructional DVD *Terrifying Guitar Trip* (Gilbert, 1995) [video] demonstrates the ease of his performance. Michael Angelo Batio's double-neck guitar shred, depicted in the video tutorial *Speed Kills* (2003) [video], does not give the impression that playing on two or four guitar necks is challenging. Decisive for virtuosity is that the mastery required to overcome difficulties needs to be apparent, yet visible technical challenges must not distract from aesthetic enjoyment (Heister, 2004: 26). Musicologist Hans-Werner Heister (2004: 22–3) distinguishes between two kinds of difficulties: the exoteric one apparent to everyone, and the esoteric one noticeable only to experts. Fans of virtuosic music are likely attracted by the second kind, as they are given an example of effortless mastery. It also fills the aspiring guitarist with awe, as is to be expected from a role model and icon (Huron, 2007). The progressive metal band Dream Theater present a good example. They are a collective of virtuosos, showing the audience that what is heard on the record can be performed with similar perfection live on stage (Custodis, 2017: 49). Recognition of esoteric difficulty contributes to the band's popularity. Musicologist Michael Custodis (2017: 49) argues that Dream Theater's virtuosity creates a connection with their audience, rather than distance; the same may apply to other guitar virtuosos discussed herein. Since live performances by instrumental rock artists have been rare (Walser, 1992: 299), especially for Shrapnel guitarists in the 1980s and 1990s (Wiederhorn, 2015), instructional videos demonstrating and explaining virtuosity allowed performers to appear approachable and human – one of the primary reasons why members of the guitar scene felt connected to virtuosos. Before the Internet made VHS and DVD media dispensable, videos of instruction and (live) performances were an important medium in the scene.

In terms of technological innovation and extending the tonal spectrum, guitarists from the heyday of shred may have contributed less than those that came before them. While known players undoubtedly contributed to progressing technology, the advances likely concerned playing, especially modifying and adopting playing techniques, along with faster speeds. Typical were creative uses of effects pedals, such as Steve Vai's use of a harmoniser in 'Ballerina 12/24' (Vai, 1990a) [audio], but few were as influential as Hendrix's sonic explorations. Guitarists such as John Petrucci used extensive rack systems and stereo effects, but such rigs improved sound quality rather than advancing music. Tom Morello is one of the few players represented in the various canons of the greatest players of all time who innovated the instrument's sonic capabilities. Best known for his music with Rage Against the Machine and Audioslave, Rensen and Stösser (2011: 217–8) name him as the most significant innovator since Eddie Van Halen. Morello was a 'virtuoso of sound' (Waksman, 2003: 132), adding new sounds to rock, such as DJ-like turntable scratches and toggle switch effects on 'Bulls on Parade' (Rage Against the Machine, 1996) [audio], funky laser blasts on 'Killing in the Name' (Rage Against the Machine, 1992b) [audio], and dramatic divebombs on 'Fistful of Steel' (Rage Against the Machine, 1992a) [audio]. Kitts and Tolinski (2002: 13) recognise him for his 'non-guitarlike sounds', some of which sound like a computer. Morello took aspiration from virtuosos such as Randy Rhoads, Nuno Bettencourt, and Eddie Van Halen and employed many contemporary techniques, yet for *The Mystique* (2019) it was his 'melting-pot guitar sound' that influenced a new age of musicians.

Morello is one of the most visible guitarists of the 1990s. His original approach to virtuosity fits the change in mainstream musical culture, moving away from heavy metal, with its fast solos, and towards grunge and alternative rock, which offer less room for virtuosity (Waksman, 2003: 128). Labels important for the widespread cultivation of shred and guitar virtuosity declined. Even though guitar virtuosity, benefitting from achievements between 1980 and 2000, became unfashionable in the mainstream (Lalaina, 2008: 74), it has continued in niche communities in the twenty-first century.

6 Guitar Technology, Playing, and Culture in the Twenty-First Century

Since the beginning of the twenty-first century, developments in the electric guitar have affected all areas: mechanical approaches to playing the instrument, exploration of technologies, places of performance, and overarching musical culture. Musicologists Slaven and Krout (2016) claim that playing has not substantially changed since the 1950s; this section argues otherwise, examining advancements of both hands in terms of picking, legato, and percussive techniques. Further discussions revolve around equipment, creativity and musicianship, and virtuosity in the twenty-first century.

6.1 Technological Innovations in Guitars and Amplifiers

Instrument modification has accompanied the development of the electric guitar in many respects. The first generation of rock guitar heroes had a particularly large share in it. Advances in their playing accompanied attempts to adapt their gear to their artistic aspirations. Such tinkering allows musicians to customise tone and reshape instruments according to their specifications. Eddie Van Halen is an often-cited case in point. As the standard features of the two renowned guitar models, Fender Stratocaster and Gibson Les Paul, were not to his liking, Van Halen created the superstrat model, which became one of the most popular designs from the 1980s onwards (Tolinski, 2017; Waksman, 2004). Music technology scholar Paul Théberge (1997: 191) has described the personalisation of tone as one of the driving forces in popular music practice. In his endeavour for an individual sound, Van Halen tinkered with his guitars and amplifiers to create a setup that supported his virtuosic playing. Guitar scholar Waksman (2004: 696–7) suggests that associating virtuosity with mastery of playing technique is too narrow. He argues that while technical mastery in the sense of craftsmanship is not a prerequisite for a virtuoso, the 'most skilled tinkerers are themselves virtuosi of a sort, having mastered the subtle process of making technological adjustments to achieve the desired result' (Waksman, 2004: 697). Either standing alongside or being part of the conventional understanding of virtuosity is what allows recognition of a 'virtuosity of sound' (Waksman, 2003: 132). The guitar discourse suggests that for several of the most influential guitarists – Eddie Van Halen, Steve Vai, and Tom Morello – both kinds of virtuosity belong together: exploration of sound and progress in playing go hand in hand.

We have found that, following a period of significant tinkering from the 1960s to the 1980s, many virtuosic guitarists in the 1990s concentrated on their playing skills rather than the instrument's development. In the new millennium, instrument and amplification technology moved to the fore. The extended-range guitar was one of the most impactful inventions, offering affordances for composition and playing styles. In the 1970s and 1980s, Uli Jon Roth experimented with extra frets to extend the instrument's pitch range upwards (Reyes, 2020: 7), and in the 1980s Steve Vai convinced Ibanez to mass-produce a seven-string version of his signature guitar with an additional lower string (Tolinski, 2017: 273). He figured that such an extension would open up a world of possibilities for rock and metal music (Vai, 2010). It took several more years before such models were produced on a larger scale. Vai's seven-string Universe model UV7 reached a wider audience through its use on the popular albums *Awake* (Dream Theater, 1994a) [audio], *Demanufacture* (Fear Factory, 1995) [audio], and *Life Is Peachy* (Korn, 1996) [audio] (Bitoun, 2018: 199). Korn's guitarist, James 'Munky' Shaffer, chose the seven-string guitar for its distinct rhythmic quality (Ibanez Guitar, 2014). The progressive proto-djent metal band Meshuggah popularised the seven-string guitar in the 1990s with their rhythmically complex performances (Gil, 2014). In the early 2000s, Meshuggah experimented with down-tuning to F (44 Hz), which resulted in their signature eight-string Ibanez model RG2228 in 2007. Following Meshuggah's tonal explorations, down-tuned seven-string guitars and later eight- and nine-string instruments became popular in the djent movement from the mid-2000s onwards, with influential bands such as Periphery, Animals as Leaders, and TesseracT inspiring a new generation of players (Bienstock, 2019c). *Guitar World* sees Animal as Leaders' guitarist Tosin Abasi as the 'leading figure and undisputed champion of the eight-string guitar' (Gil, 2014: 10). Abasi took Vai's vision of what extended-range guitars could offer to a new level. These instruments allowed him to harness a rhythmic 'thumping' technique (see Section 6.2) and play complex chords, multi-finger tapping, eight-string sweep picking, and forms of soloing that transcend genre boundaries. This intertwined development of technique and technology has earned him widespread recognition, as exemplified by a *Guitar World* accolade: 'He takes everything we think we know and understand about the instrument and twists it into something dizzyingly new' (Bienstock, 2019c). After playing two signature eight-string guitars from Ibanez, Abasi founded Abasi Concepts, a guitar company that followed the tradition of tinkering, offering 'visionary players the creative tools to break boundaries', 'new realms of sound, responsiveness or ergonomics', and 'exceptional sonic depth and playability' (Abasi Concepts, 2020). Many contemporary virtuosos play extended-range guitars for their potential to broaden solo and rhythm playing styles and for tonal reasons, with metal musicians especially striving for ever-lower timbres (Herbst, 2017a). Smaller boutique companies such as Strandberg are popular with virtuosos. Ibanez, Jackson, ESP, and Schecter are among the major guitar manufacturers now offering eight-string guitars, mainly aimed at the metal community. A recent trend is nine-string guitars with a third lower string that reaches C# (35 Hz). How these guitars sound can be heard on 'Private Visions of the World' (Animals as Leaders, 2016) [audio] and 'The Husk' (Rings of Saturn, 2019) [audio].

In terms of amplification, rock guitarists have long resisted serious innovation and stuck with valve amplifiers. Even modern models differ only slightly from those of the 1960s and 1970s (Herbst, 2019a). Transistor-based amplification has largely been rejected for its perceived lack of warmth and for ideological reasons, adhering to traditional technologies and sounds (Herbst, 2019b; Herbst, Czedik-Eysenberg, & Reuter, 2018). The standard, especially in recorded rock and metal music, is still the traditional way of capturing the tone of a valve amplifier through a cabinet picked up by a microphone (Mynett, 2017: 57). Nevertheless, many contemporary guitar virtuosos have freed themselves from this longstanding practice and its drawbacks for live performance: namely, being difficult to transport, prone to errors, loud stage levels, varying front-of-house sound quality, and unpredictable tones at each venue (Herbst, 2019b; Herbst, Czedik-Eysenberg, & Reuter, 2018). Players have also turned to digital solutions in the studio for more control over tone and production aesthetics (Herbst, 2023). Popular digital hardware devices are the Line 6 Helix and Fractal Audio's Axe-FX, played by Animals as Leaders' Tosin Abasi and Javier Reyes, Periphery's Misha Mansoor, Monument's John Browne, Megadeth's Synyster Gates, and solo artists Jason Richardson and Guthrie Govan.

Virtuoso Plini admits to having used free plug-ins on his releases for economic reasons. His first three EPs were recorded in his bedroom, which did not allow him to record a high-volume valve amplifier with a microphone (Xavier, 2015). Digital amplifier simulations were adopted by progressive metal guitarists out of necessity and for aesthetic reasons. Djent guitarists have chosen freeware plug-ins for sonic or workflow reasons (Marrington, 2019; Shelvock, 2014: 134). Periphery recorded amplifier simulations on their first album (Chopik, 2012) and inspired later djent bands to follow suit. Taylor Larson, producer of Periphery's debut album and other contemporary progressive metal

acts such as Asking Alexandria and Jason Richardson, prefers amplifier simu-
lation plug-ins over recording physical amplifiers (Larson, 2017, 2018). John
Browne, one of the founding guitarists of djent, recorded the affordable Line 6
POD XT Pro amplifier simulation for all productions of his band Monuments.
He also prefers the sound of the digital unit because the exaggerated treble range
highlights playing weaknesses, which forces him to play more cleanly (Browne,
2017). Most guitarists since the 1980s have used a Tubescreamer booster
(Herbst, 2016: 83, 102). Contemporary players continue this practice (Herbst,
2019a), albeit using a virtual Tubescreamer. Whereas in the past it was
employed to increase distortion levels and tighten up the low-end of an analogue
valve amplifier (Herbst, 2019a), modern virtuosos use a booster to brighten up
the dark timbre of extended-range guitars (Shelvock, 2014: 132), improving
note definition and clarity to emphasise their technically clean playing.

Recently, there has been a shift away from freeware and affordable digital
simulations and towards sophisticated plug-ins, usually associated with known
players or producers. Metalcore producer Joey Sturgis and his company
Toneforge offer signature plug-ins by Jason Richardson and Misha Mansoor,
created in collaboration with producer Taylor Larson. They include features that
utilise the affordances of digital signal processing, such as the 'infinity gain
knob'. Unlike traditional amplifiers, these plug-ins are a virtual guitar rig
providing options for combining various elements from pre-amplifiers, power
amplifiers, and cabinets to effects, creating a 'final-mix guitar tone' (Toneforge,
2020) without the need for conventional engineering. Neural DSP offer simulations with signature plug-ins by Tosin Abasi, Plini, and Periphery's audio
engineer Adam 'Nolly' Getgood. These three simulations have in common
that they allow tonal variety at studio quality beyond what traditional analogue
valve amplifiers offer: nuanced dynamic processors, spectral controls, time
effects, and cabinet simulations. Processing, such as compression and noise
gates, which virtuosos would traditionally have rejected (Herbst, 2019a), is
accepted in the (virtual) rig and has become a standard practice of contemporary
progressive rock guitarists (Shelvock, 2014). In the past, gates and compression
were perceived as 'cheating' because they make standard techniques such as
legato easier to play through dynamic range compression (Herbst, 2017c), yet
current guitarists utilise them for multi-finger tapping techniques, where the
hands' menial function of muting strings is replaced by a more complex
coordination of playing movements. The reason is not primarily about making
the instrument easier to play but that a 'high level of dynamic range is less
desirable in progressive metal, where value is placed on technicality and precision' (Shelvock, 2014: 132). A distorted sound is less challenging to play
because distortion compresses the sound and lengthens notes, smoothing the

transition time and masking asynchronous hand coordination (Herbst, 2017b). By contrast, a clean but compressed tone amplifies noise without the beneficial smoothing effect of distortion. That is why a compressed, relatively undistorted sound requires clean technical execution, increasing playing difficulty.

Amplification simulations were initially born out of necessity to provide access to a wide range of tones in an affordable device or for playing at bedroom levels (Burns, 2016). For a long time, they were treated as a secondary solution, barely worth recording or playing on stage (Herbst, Czedik-Eysenberg, & Reuter, 2018). Progressive rock guitarists have embraced amplifier simulations to achieve a high level of sound control and create signature sounds that go hand in hand with playing (Strachan, 2017: 149). Just as Eddie Van Halen used to tinker with his guitar and amplifier to personalise his tone and create a rig that supported his original playing style (Waksman, 2004), virtuosos of the current generation actively participate in technological development for the sake of their music.

Guitar simulations used to be meticulously modelled after analogue hardware devices. Popular are Line 6 Helix, Fractal Audio Axe-FX, and the Kemper Profiling Amplifier, which produce authentic valve sounds in digital hardware units (Herbst, Czedik-Eysenberg, & Reuter, 2018). The Neural DSP Quad-Cortex is not only a digital device that emulates analogue sounds but also a hardware device that can be played on a live stage based on a computer plug-in simulation; this reverses the common practice of modelling hardware devices as software plug-ins. By taking the opportunities of digitalisation and collaborating with smaller enterprises, virtuosic guitarists of the twenty-first century are developing electric guitar technology without the ideological constraints to adhere to traditional tones that have long shaped guitar communities (Herbst, Czedik-Eysenberg, & Reuter, 2018). The complexity of digital signal processing might prove challenging for guitarists to develop technology independently. However, with their futuristic visions, and in continuation of the long-term DIY spirit, they still provide novel ideas to equipment developers. Their name on the signature device helps disseminate the technology to guitar communities, as evidenced by manufacturers' marketing campaigns and web presence.

6.2 Advances in Electric Guitar Playing

Picking

Alternate picking is a basic electric guitar technique whose principal mechanics have been only slightly modified to achieve greater economy of motion and increased speed. Guitar educator German Schauss (2017: 4) analysed the picking technique of 1980s and 1990s shredders, hoping to uncover the secrets of their great speed and precision. Given the variety of mechanics, he concluded that there might not be one best way. The only commonality he found was the synchronised coordination between both hands. This finding is consistent with the writing of virtuoso Guthrie Govan (2002b: 36–7), who sees speed as a by-product of accuracy and efficiency, achieved by minimising movement (see also Brooks, 2017). Another ergonomic improvement is the slanting of the pick (Figure 27), which prevents the plectrum from attacking the string while it is completely perpendicular to the string ('flat-picking'). The pick is angled so there is less friction, allowing the plectrum to glide easily over the string (Vallejo, 2020: 28). Pick-slanting is commonly used in conjunction with edge-picking (Figure 28): the tilting of the pick to a 45-degree angle to attack the string with the edge, further reducing friction (Petrucci, 2016) [video].

Speed fascinates many rock guitarists, as exemplified by a popular thread with 3,349 posts between May 2006 and October 2013 on the *Ultimate Guitar* (2006) forum that compares the notes per second per artist alongside the playing technique, unveiling the fastest guitarist (see https://tinyurl.com/2p968s4a). Such statistics disregard that playing difficulty depends on many variables, such as note choice, phrase length, guitar tone, and the wider arrangement exposing or hiding sloppi-ness. It thus seems futile to compare the top speeds of contemporary virtuosos with earlier shredders. Comparing Paul Gilbert's 'Scarified' (Racer X, 1987a) [audio], Rusty Cooley's 'Under the Influence' (Cooley, 2002b) [audio], and Jason Richardson's 'Hos Down' (Richardson, 2016a) [audio] exposes a gradual develop-ment of playing with cleaner execution rather than significantly increased maximum speed. Moreover, melodic fragments have changed from three-note-per-string scalar runs (Alexander, 2018: 33) to wider intervals, which are challenging to play because they are harder to execute with conventional techniques (see Section 5.2). In popular guitar discourse, contemporary players are recognised

Figure 27 Downward pick-slanting

Figure 28 Edge-picking

for cleanliness, speed, and difficult melody lines. According to *Guitar World*, Jason Richardson is one of today's prime shredders, who 'plays insanely technical and blindingly fast runs with a precision and cleanliness that is practically superhuman' (Bienstock, 2019c). *Music Radar* similarly notes that in a 'post-Gilbert/Petrucci/Govan world of technical virtuosity, it seems there are still new levels of speed and stamina to achieve and Jason [Richardson] is proud to pursue them' (Sidwell, 2018). 'Hos Down' (Richardson, 2016a) demonstrates Richardson's alternate picking speed and cleanliness.

The academic discussion suggests that sweep picking developed little further until the mid-1980s. The history of this technique points to different approaches to the picking hand. A recent approach is adjusting the fretting hand for cleaner results. Yngwie Malmsteen was among the few players in the 1980s who avoided barring the strings when playing notes on the same fret across multiple strings (Figure 29) (Brooks, 2017: 114). Shredders in the 1990s, like Rusty Cooley, followed this tradition.

Cooley stated he would do 'anything ... to get away from barring' (Shred Guitar TV, 2019). However, he used barring only for arpeggio shapes on three and four strings; otherwise, he played five and six-string arpeggios by rolling his fingers across several strings. According to Jason Richardson, such rolling allows for inconsistencies when trying to avoid overlapping notes:

> I exclude barring from virtually all triadic shapes when playing ascending and descending arpeggios on every part of the fretboard. I feel that omitting barring helps tremendously in eliminating any possibility of two notes ringing together while moving from note to note through the arpeggio shapes. The literal definition of an arpeggio is a 'broken chord', so none of the notes are supposed to ring simultaneously. (Richardson, in *Total Guitar*, 2020)

Besides barring and rolling the fingers, Richardson alternates fingers on the same fret on different strings to minimise the risk of overlapping notes, which

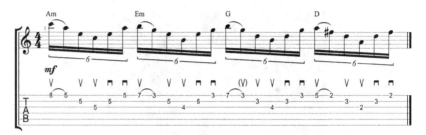

Figure 29 Sweeping section where the arpeggios Am and G involve potential barring of the index finger

would create an interval instead of an arpeggio. Like Cooley, Richardson admits that sometimes there is no ergonomic way to perform a sweep without barring. Richardson's clean approach to sweeping can be heard on his guest solo on 'Nasty' (Polyphia, 2018a) [audio 2:42–3:12].

Another development in sweeping is the adaptation to extended-range guitars. Neoclassical shredder Joe Stump suggests that increasing the number of strings has long been the main advancement in sweeping technique:

> It's funny: many of today's younger players are more familiar with larger arpeggio shapes (five/six-string arpeggios) than smaller ones. Meanwhile, back when I first started to play and learn arpeggio shapes/sequences, those larger shapes weren't nearly as common, and the two-string arpeggio was a real staple of every hard rock/metal player's vocabulary. All of the European hard rock/metal masters that influenced me tremendously (Ritchie Blackmore, Uli Jon Roth, Michael Schenker, Gary Moore, and later on Yngwie Malmsteen) predominantly used smaller two- and three-string arpeggios. It wasn't until Yngwie and then Michael Angelo Batio . . . that the larger shapes became more prominent. (Stump, 2017: 1)

Jason Becker made a name for himself as a sweep expert by using five- and six-string arpeggios (George, 2019: 39; Govan, 2002a: 40; Thorpe, 2016: 19; Zoupa, 2018: 104), as heard in 'Altitudes' (Becker, 1988a) [audio 1:58–2:24]. In the early 2000s, virtuosos such as Jeff Loomis explored six and seven-string arpeggio shapes (Thorpe, 2016: 51; 2019: 89) – for example, on 'Psalm of Lydia' (Nevermore, 2005) [audio 0:17–0:28, video]. More recently, players such as Tosin Abasi have turned to lower register sweeps on seven- and eight-string guitars (Figure 30). Since such low notes lack clarity, contemporary players make a point of articulating them clearly through pick slanting. Furthermore, the lowest notes are sometimes palm-muted, as on 'Mind-Spun' (Animals as Leaders, 2014a) [audio 0:45–1:15, video 0:37–1:08], to increase note definition (Herbst, 2017b), something that was rarely done before.

Figure 30 Sweeping in 'Mind Spun'

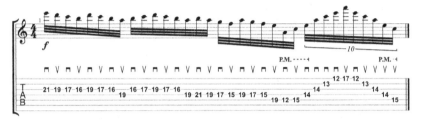

Figure 31 Transitional sweeping in 'Hos Down'

Contemporary guitarists using sweeping rarely dedicate entire sections to this technique, as was common practice in the 1980s and 1990s. Rather, it is intended as a seasoning because long sweeping sections are regarded as a cliché to be avoided (Zoupa, 2018: 88). There are exceptions, however, like Polyphia's '40oz' (Polyphia, 2017) [audio 0:26–0:53, video 0:34–1:17] with longer sweep-picked sections, notably played with a clean guitar tone, but even those are slower and serve a different compositional purpose. For example, sweeping can be used for transitions between sections, as in 'Hos Down' (Richardson, 2016a) [audio 0:41–0:43] (Figure 31), and to outline arpeggios, as in 'Welcome to the Wasteland' (Helfrich, 2016) [audio 2:01–2:14]. Often combined in musical phrases consisting of different playing techniques, sweeping is employed for showmanship, a burst of energy, or as a transitional tool to bridge music sections. The main development in sweeping, like alternate picking, is cleanliness, accuracy, and compositional use instead of higher playing speed.

Legato

Basic legato playing has developed with only a few mechanical tweaks since the 1980s. For example, contemporary legato player Tom Quayle (2020a) recommends not planting the index finger on the fretboard. He believes that this 'lazy finger syndrome' [video] holds back legato playing, a problem that could be avoided by lifting the finger in question, even if the player uses it again on the same fret in a legato line.

The most significant development in legato playing concerns tapping. From the 1980s onwards, guitarists like Eddie Van Halen, Kirk Hammett, Randy Rhoads, and Nuno Bettencourt employed this technique with several fingers of both hands to play notes faster on a single string, as heard in Van Halen's 'Eruption' (Van Halen, 1978b) [audio 0:57–1:23] and Metallica's 'One' (Metallica, 1988) [audio 5:46–5:53]. Contemporary guitarists follow this approach but employ tapping for large intervallic leaps in a melodic context. An example is Jason Richardson's 'Omni' (Richardson, 2016b) [audio 0:34–1:07, video 0:34–1:07], where tapping is utilised to play the riff's main motif rather than a fast solo technique (Figure 32).

Richardson uses more than one finger of the picking hand to play across several strings with greater freedom, contrasting older shred-style tapping licks. This multi-finger tapping has already been employed by Eddie Van Halen, Steve Vai (Govan, 2002a: 68), Joe Satriani (Schauss, 2012: 95), Michael Romeo (Dillard, 2007: 74), Night Ranger's Jeff Watson (*Guitar World*, 2015), and by Michael Jackson's long-time guitarist Jennifer Batten (Dillard, 2007: 74). Multi-finger tapping can be applied in a linear way on one string, for example, to shift from three notes played with the fretting hand and one with the picking hand to a two-and-two articulation, using two different fingers of the picking hand (Neyens, 2020: 65). Such linear tapping is possible across different strings, of which the arpeggiated run in Govan's 'Wonderful Slippery Thing' (Govan, 2006c) [audio 1:22–1:27, video 1:22–1:27] is an example. Here, tapping is intended to remove the slightly percussive sound of sweep-picked arpeggios (see Section 5.2).

Linear multi-finger tapping is defined by both hands sharing the same role in developing arpeggios, melodies, and complex textural passages (Vallejo, 2020: 43–5). In the most sophisticated way, eight fingers are used (four from each hand). As virtuoso Govan notes, this technique is most associated with metal guitar playing but allows for 'piano-like chord voicings and cascading scale

Figure 32 Main tapping motif in 'Omni'

Figure 33 Linear multi-finger tapping in 'Mindful Madness'

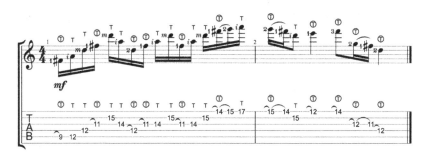

Figure 34 Stacking in 'Tydes'

runs that sound great with a clean tone' (Govan, 2002a: 9). For this effect, it is popular with many contemporary performers outside the metal genre, such as Sarah Longfield, Josh Martin, and Dan James Griffin (Neyens, 2020), as heard as on 'Mindful Madness' (Griffin, 2017) (Figure 33) [audio, video].

A specific application of this technique by players such as Griffin and Longfield is 'stacking' (Vallejo, 2020: 43), where part of a melody line, scale, or arpeggio is tapped with alternating hands, for example on 'Tydes' (Longfield, 2017) (Figure 34) [audio 0:37–0:55, video 0:29–0:48]. It is noteworthy that in contrast to the heavily distorted guitar tones of the 1980s used for tapping, many contemporary guitarists play a clean or slightly crunched tone, as demonstrated on 'Nero' (Covet, 2020) [audio 0:20–0:42, video 2:57–4:08].

A yet more advanced form of multi-finger tapping is 'multi-role' or 'pianistic' tapping, with both hands sharing responsibility for harmony and melody (Vallejo, 2020: 45–7). It is not an entirely new technique, having already been performed on the guitar in the 1980s, for example, by Stanley Jordan (Turner, 2015: 64–5). Jordan's fretting hand mainly plays the lower strings with the chords and bass lines, occasionally creating harmonies with the main melody, while the picking hand plays the melodies. There are basic approaches to pianistic tapping, where the picking hand carries the melody while the fretting hand holds the harmony, working together instead of having independent roles. Rob Scallon's 'For That Second' (Scallon, 2014) [audio, video] is an example of this approach (Figure 35).

Contemporary players such as Ichika Nito, Mateus Asato, and Ant Law build on Jordan's explorations, creating more complex arrangements with more sophisticated polyphony (Sidwell, 2018; *Total Guitar*, 2020). Yvette Young of Covet has been exploring the potential of this technically demanding approach over the past five years, transferring pianistic polyphony and combined harmony and melody playing to the guitar. Young uses open tunings in most songs. The guitar is tuned to an open chord, such as DADGAD (Dsus4 tuning), or other harmonically unrelated alternate tunings like FACGBE (Neyens, 2020: 74–5). On 'Nautilus' (Covet, 2016) [audio, video], this technique is applied throughout the song, and is most apparent in the first section (Figure 36). The bass notes are played by the fretting hand, but both hands share the rest of the melody and inner voices. Marcos Mena of Standards is another guitarist known for this approach.

'Special Berry' (Standards, 2020) [audio, video] features multi-role tapping prominently. Mena also uses a technique called 'cross-tapping' (Vallejo 2020: 47), where both hands cross each other to reach notes otherwise unattainable.

Guitar manuals highlight Josh Martin of Little Tybee for setting a benchmark in current tapping practice. He develops various styles that bring percussive elements to a technique that traditionally focuses on melody and harmony (Neyens, 2020: 82–4; Zoupa, 2018: 88). Martin made 'butterfly tapping' and 'glitch tapping' better known (Neyens, 2020: 82–3; Vallejo, 2020: 47–8). 'Butterfly tapping' means the guitarist taps the frets in different rhythms, usually at a fast pace to create a staccato flutter effect (Martin, 2017), which can be heard on various songs by Little Tybee, including 'Left Right' (Little Tybee, 2013b) [audio 2:18–2:50, video 0:21–0:53]. The technique requires holding a chord shape in the fretting hand while the extension of the chord is played by the picking hand. These shapes are tapped alternately with

Figure 35 Pianistic tapping in 'For That Second'; all notes are played legato

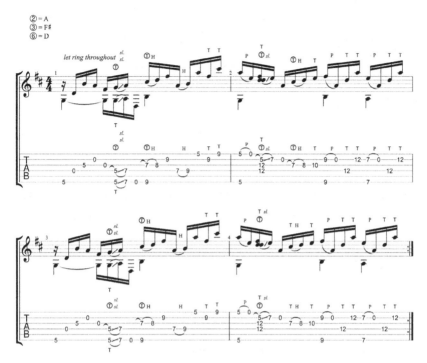

Figure 36 Multi-role tapping in 'Nautilus' with bass, harmony, and melody layers

polyrhythms and rhythmic patterns (Figure 37), adopted from drumming techniques such as single stroke rolls (alternating left and right hand) and paradiddles (left, right, left, left, followed by right, left, right, right).

'Glitch tapping' is another percussive approach to tapping that produces a stutter effect and adds rhythmic interest to melodic lines (Martin, 2015b) [video]. It is performed by tapping the same fret on the same string with multiple fingers in quick succession, creating a 'glitchy' sound that can be heard on Little Tybee's 'Hearing Blue' (Little Tybee, 2013a) [audio 4:33–4:48, video 4:36–4:52]. Although a niche technique, glitch tapping has gained popularity for its qualities of rhythmic layering in compositions. It creates interesting groove patterns whilst carrying the harmony, and it can be utilised as a rhythmic and harmonic foundation of a piece. Still another development within tapping is 'under-strumming' (Martin, 2015a) [video], where the fingers and thumb of the picking hand strum underneath the note already tapped. The second section of 'Languid' (Little Tybee, 2016) [audio 2:52–4:14, video 3:04–4:05] builds on this technique, mixed with flamenco rasgueado technique. Altogether, tapping techniques are nowadays used for ergonomic reasons when dealing with large

Figure 37 Butterfly tapping in 'Left Right'

intervallic leaps, along with compositional motivations such as controlling the entire harmony, creating unconventional textures, and developing rhythmic interest.

Thumping

Other instruments have been sources of inspiration for some of the most innovative musicians in the history of electric guitar playing. Percussive techniques have been explored, such as Van Halen's 'slap-tapping' on 'Spanish Fly' (Van Halen, 1979) [audio 0:00–0:10, video 0:05–0:20] and Buckethead's slap-bass techniques on 'Robot Transmission' (Buckethead, 1996) [audio]. Inspired by Chapman Stick players like Tony Levitin and funk bassists Jaco Pastorius and Rocco Prestia, Guthrie Govan has experimented with slapping the strings with both hands to build speed and create a percussive 'finger funk sound' (Govan, 2002a: 104–6). In the twenty-first century, this percussive approach has been developed further in the form of 'thumping'. Despite its brief history, thumping has become more common in recent years (Abasi, 2020; Astley-Brown, 2020b). Technically, the picking hand's thumb is pushed through a string like a bassist would slap, but immediately after, the thumb is brought back up through the string. Bassist Victor Wooten inspired this double-thump (Figure 38), according to thumping populariser Tosin Abasi [video]. After the double-thump, the guitarist may pluck other notes with the picking-hand fingers while maintaining the thumping position. It is a weaker form of the bass guitar's 'popping' technique and more like fingerstyle plucking, similar to the tremolo technique of the classical guitar, though with a percussive twist (see Vallejo, 2020: 58–67).

Thumping on the guitar was popularised through Tosin Abasi's music and comprehensive course with *Guitar Messenger*, 'Thump!' (Abasi, 2020) [video]. However, other guitarists had used this technique before him, as evidenced by an amateur video from 1995 in which Scotty Mishoe plays the slapping and popping technique on guitar (bestguitarvids, 2011) [video]. Contemporary adopters of the technique include Josh Martin, Tim Henson, Josh Martin,

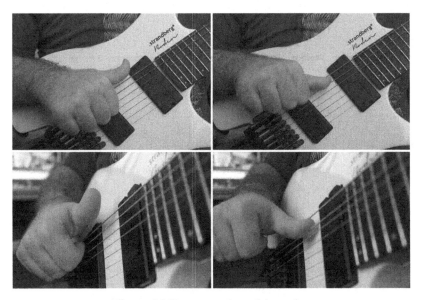

Figure 38 Demonstration of thumping

Kevin Blake Goodwin, Jose Macario, and Javier Reyes. Most guitarists tend to thump on extended-range guitars because the percussive sound is clearer in the lower register. Thumping is increasingly used on traditional six-string guitars, as on 'Special Berry' (Standards, 2020) [audio, video].

Abasi (2020) explains in his instructional video that a specific guitar tone is required to fully utilise the thumping technique. Guitarists must attain a controlled sound, achieved by using one or several noise gates. Another key component is a compressor to keep the attack and volume constant in fast sections. For amplification, Abasi recommends blending two devices with different character-istics: one with crunch for attack and punch, and another for low-end clarity and power to create a clear yet aggressive tone. Single coil or other pickups that allow the player to coil tap are preferable, as they give guitarists a lower output that complements the technique with a percussive attack quality (Abasi, 2020).

Regarding musical application, thumping allows the creation of rhythmic foundations and layering, bridging melodic and percussive parts. It is used as a textural tool and can be combined with other techniques, such as hammer-on legato or fingerstyle approaches typical of the classical guitar [video]. Notes are added for harmonic enrichment next to accentuation. In a rhythmic context, the thumb usually strikes first to play a note, followed by muting to create emphasis to outline a grouping, as heard on 'The Woven Web' (Animals as Leaders, 2014b) [audio 1:28–2:01, video 1:16–1:50]. In this example, the articulated notes are placed towards the end of groupings for syncopation (Figure 39).

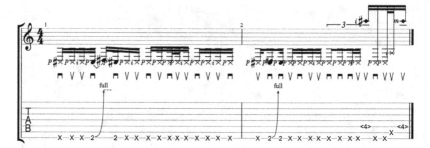

Figure 39 Thumping in 'Woven Web'; letters denote fingers: p (thumb), i (index), and m (middle)

Thumping facilitates outlining arpeggios or creating melodic lines in the guitar's upper register while maintaining the percussive attack of the technique. A continuous percussive pedal can be kept, with the fingers performing more melodic components of the music. These applications are apparent in various Animals as Leaders' songs, including 'An Infinite Regression' (Animals as Leaders, 2011) [audio, video]. As an unconventional approach to rhythm and lead playing, thumping has gained popularity and become part of the skill set of many virtuosic guitarists, such as Josh Martin (2020) and Tim Henson (Astley-Brown, 2020b).

6.3 Twenty-First Century Electric Guitar Virtuosity

Academic discussions of virtuosity generally revolve more around solo playing and performance than accompaniment and composition (Heister, 2004). Common understanding of virtuosity encompasses the technique, speed, and physical dexterity of a performer (Hennion, 2012). In some guitar scenes, however, virtuosity extends to other areas, increasingly including creativity in songwriting and the ability to record, mix, master, and produce music. Many shredders of the 1980s were perceived as being poor rhythm players. They were accused of the 'sin' of virtuosity (Fellezs, 2018; Waksman, 2003; Walser, 1992), which suggests that their compositions were of low quality, primarily intended to show off technique. In contrast, it appears that many contemporary guitarists view their virtuosity as an interconnected combination of the playing skills needed for both traditional lead and song-oriented rhythm playing. Technological considerations are incorporated into tones that maximise the intended playing aesthetic but are also used as creative compositional tools. Besides, while virtuosity in rock music of the 1980s and 1990s was mainly associated with shredding, many contemporary virtuosos seek inspiration outside this genre.

Virtuosity, Creativity, And Songwriting

The motivation for adding strings, which resulted in the now popular extended-range guitars, may have stemmed from the desire to explore rhythm playing, as the early albums in the 1990s popularising these instruments suggest (see Section 6.1). On the one hand, musicians wanted to produce deeper timbres without needing to down-tune their guitars (Gil, 2014). On the other hand, such deep timbres lend themselves to more percussive playing styles (Shelvock, 2014). Consequently, progressive metal and math rock guitarists, in particular, generated a form of rhythmic virtuosity with odd time signatures and groupings, polyrhythms, and other complex rhythmic subdivisions, as exemplified by 'An Infinite Regression' (Animals as Leaders, 2011) [audio, video]. Such rhythm parts also required an adjustment in playing technique. Extended-range guitarists play palm-muting differently, moving the palm slightly towards the bridge pickup to create a more percussive and transient-rich tone. To emphasise this effect and to improve note clarity, they slant their pick more than the average guitarist does (Shelvock, 2014: 129). In addition to modifications of picking in rhythm guitar playing, bands such as Periphery, Plini, and Animals as Leaders use jazz-inspired chords that add harmonic complexity to their compositions (*Total Guitar*, 2020).

Almost all analysed guitar instructional books, including those aimed at aspiring virtuosos, emphasise that playing technique is not an end in itself, as it must serve a musical purpose. Kristof Neyens (2020: 4) and Chris Zoupa (2018: 88) are suspicious of advanced techniques such as eight-finger tapping because they can be played with bad taste. For example, virtuoso-educator Govan (2002a: 57) has called tapping a 'much-maligned aspect of guitar playing' for its uninspired and overly indulgent use in shredding. As the preceding discussions have shown (Section 6.2), contemporary guitarists have developed forms of polyphonic and percussive tapping that are harnessed as expressive tools and for songwriting purposes. Guitar media portrays many current virtuosos as not seeing themselves primarily as guitarists but as musicians and composers who put technique at the service of their music (Astley-Brown, 2019c; Bienstock, 2020). Regardless of how technically proficient a performer is, their creative merits in composing and improvising are relevant in gaining recognition, as is a sense of style and tone. In the words of Guthrie Govan, 'The older, wiser player knows in a deep, intuitive way that it's the quality of the playing that counts: does it have a decent tone? Is it a beautiful sound and are you putting it in exactly the right place relative to the pulse of the music?' (Marten, 2018). Some highly successful bands, such as Polyphia, claim to avoid using advanced techniques to display pure physical virtuosity (Astley-Brown, 2019c) and instead subscribe to the phrase 'less is more', contrary to older views such as Yngwie Malmsteen's mantra 'more is more' (Dunn, 2010).

Structures, harmony, and songwriting vary considerably between contemporary virtuosic rock and metal artists. Plini (2019) and Yvette Young (Li, 2021), for example, compose their music note by note (Plini, 2019), whereas solo artist Nick Johnston leaves space for improvisation (*MyGuitarLessons*, 2017). Aaron Marshall of the progressive metal band Intervals structures his music like a pop song (Mary, 2014). Solo artist Dan James Griffin spices his compositions with electronic ingredients, as on 'Snowdrift' (Griffin, 2021) [audio], and progressive rock outlet Polyphia use their guitars as tools for electronic and hip-hop-inspired creations, exemplified by 'Drown' (Polyphia, 2018d) [audio]. Some musicians, such as Sarah Longfield [video], Yvette Young [video piano, video violin], Dan James Griffins [video], and Kevin Blade Goodwin [video], do not limit themselves to the guitar but are multi-instrumentalists and utilise live electronics such as modular synthesisers, looping devices, and turntables in their performances and creations. Overall, the current approach to music-making is multifaceted and increasingly crosses genre boundaries in terms of structure, instrumentation, harmony, and timbre. Rock and metal elements are blended with electronic dance music, drum and bass, indie, and mainstream pop music.

Most contemporary rock guitarists acknowledged by popular guitar media (see Section 2) are progressive artists, especially in djent, a modern metal subgenre. Genre classifications are debated within the scene, where some prefer the label 'progressive' to progressive rock or metal, as does Tosin Abasi:

> There are prog metal and prog rock, which is actually not as progressive as the title would suggest. Legitimately, it's almost like a snapshot of the progenitors of progressive rock. So you have your casts and your genesis, and it's almost like as a producer, you're going to hear certain synth generations, you're going to hear certain types of tones in the palette that represent the genesis of prog. And I think people carry that tradition. And that's when you say prog – you kind-of refer to that. Then there's progressive like as a fundamental approach which doesn't have those parameters – it's whatever you want it to be. (Abasi, in Beato, 2020)

Abasi prefers the label 'progressive' because the variety of sounds in virtuosic guitar music, including electronic sounds and the aesthetics of computer-produced music, would not allow for an encapsulating term that defines the genre. For example, Polyphia have been referred to as the 'Limp Bizkit of modern prog' (Neely, 2020). On their latest album, *New Levels New Devils* (Polyphia, 2018b) [audio], a marked influence from mainstream pop is evident in terms of structure, timbral choices, and electronic percussion, whilst maintaining the complexity of progressive rock (Astley-Brown, 2019c). Polyphia see the guitar not as an instrument to express virtuosity but as a tool to create music (Astley-Brown, 2019c). Speaking about 'O.D.' (Polyphia, 2018c) [audio], guitarist Tim Henson (2020a) reveals that the main influence for the song's chord choice and beat making stemmed from 'Champions' (West, 2016) [audio] by Kanye West, and the structure from 'Look What You Made Me Do' (Swift, 2017) [audio] by Taylor Swift; Henson liked the structure and adopted it with a few changes. 'O.D.' also features electronic drum kits and 808 bass sounds throughout, along with effects-heavy guitar lines.

Amongst the guitarists influenced by electronically driven genres are Dan James Griffin, Oyvind 'Owane' Pedersen, and Jacob 'Quist' Quistgaard. Although electronic sounds such as synthesisers and electronic percussion are popular, other genres can be inspirational too. Aaron Marshall of Intervals is inspired by bands from the pop-punk era of the early 2000s, such as Green Day, and their melodic approach to rock (D'Addario, 2019), as can be heard in '5-HTP' (Intervals, 2020) [audio]. Yvette Young, a pianist-guitarist, states 'I never really listen to guitar music, so I only listen to bands and composers' (Astley-Brown, 2019c). Her approach to tapping on the guitar is inspired by the piano: 'The two-handed tapping I play, I approach the guitar just how I'd approach writing polyphony on a piano. I started playing the way I play because I didn't have a band; I just wanted to sound as full as possible by myself' (Astley-Brown, 2019c). 'Nautilus' (Covet, 2016) [audio] exemplifies her style. Plini, on the other hand, is mainly influenced by classic shredders such as John Petrucci, Steve Vai, and Joe Satriani (McAllister, 2020), as illustrated on his most recent album (Plini, 2020a) [audio]. Jason Richardson cites John Petrucci as his idol (Bienstock, 2019a). Jack Gardiner and Tosin Abasi similarly draw inspiration from other guitarists, such as fusion players Tom Quayle and Guthrie Govan, but primarily from Allan Holdsworth (Beato, 2020). The approach to harmony in the guitar-led community encompasses a wide range, from basic cadential chord progressions to symmetrical scales and the modes of the melodic major scale. The harmonic influence depends on the respective artist and their influences. Two examples are Guthrie Govan, who inspired Jack Gardiner's modal playing, and Allan Holdsworth, who inspired Tosin Abasi's use of altered, augmented, and harmonic major scales (Beato, 2020).

The advent of guitar-specific notation software fundamentally changed songwriting. Such software is popular with guitarists as it allows them to practice their compositional skills away from the guitar. Guitar Pro is a tablature software that promotes both compositional and physical skills. In an interview, Jason Richardson explains that writing music without the instrument in his hand helps him break out of routines and avoid standard licks. He admits that writing the solo for 'Behold' (Born of Osiris, 2011) [audio 3:40–4:08] in Guitar Pro forced him to learn something new, which developed his compositional reper-toire and playing technique (Grunwald, 2011). Even though Guitar Pro facili-tates the creation of complex melodic content, artists such as Aaron Marshall, Plini, Jack Gardiner, and Sithu Aye write melodic material intended as hooks, regardless of whether their music is based on mainstream structures. The current generation of band guitarists must think about their role in the arrange-ment, in contrast to solo artists. For Marshall, 'the music that excels, or shines the most, is the stuff that considers the rest of the band . . . drums are, I would say, the most important thing in terms of dictating how the composition moves' (D'Addario, 2019). Guitar-led music of today involves, in the rarest of cases, merely a guitarist and a backing track.

Perfection, Authenticity, and Ethics

Along with technical accomplishments, the need for authenticity is also grow-ing. Musicians have long been suspected of 'touching up' their performances on recordings (Grossberg, 1992: 208). An example from the technical metal scene is Dragonforce; they were accused of recording the solos on their debut album *Valley of the Damned* (Dragonforce, 2002) [audio] note for note and artificially speeding them up (Seth, 2017). As guitar scholar Waksman notes, 'rock guitar has assumed an almost "traditionalist" aura for many audiences and musicians, encased in a nostalgia for past forms that in previous eras was reserved for more folk-based styles of expression' (Waksman, 2003: 131). In rock and related guitar scenes, authenticity of expression (Moore, 2002), unmediated by techno-logical trickery or fakery, is essential. The live show has served as evidence of authentic expression, according to Lawrence Grossberg: 'The importance of live performances [in rock] lies precisely in the fact that it is only here that one can see the actual production of the sound, and the emotional work carried in the voice. The demand for live performance has always expressed the desire for the visual mark (and proof) of authenticity' (Grossberg, 1992: 208). This line of thinking prompted Dragonforce to repeatedly refer to their live qualities in response to accusations of cheating (Seth, 2017). A review of their album *The Power Within* (Dragonforce, 2012) [audio] suggests this strategy is working: 'If you didn't know that the sextet is not slower live, you would inevitably ask yourself if they did not cheat thoroughly on this record' (Butterweck, 2012).

In the virtuosic rock guitar communities, employing tricks to gain an advan-tage over other players has long been discussed, as Herbst (2017c) finds in an empirical study of online discussions. It concludes that the main suspect of cheating is distortion due to the smoothening effect of compression, which removes some technical demands of playing legato and hand synchronisation when picking (Herbst, 2017b). The study further finds that high-output pickups and thinner gauge strings are also viewed with suspicion for reasons applying to distortion (Herbst, 2017c). Other tools potentially used for deception include hairbands, socks, and fret wraps to mute noise that must be controlled by the player (Herbst, 2017c). Using such tools may appear insignificant, but shredders such as Paul Gilbert and Jason Richardson stress that controlling unwanted noise is one of the main challenges of rock guitar playing (*Guitar World*, 2019; *Total Guitar*, 2012). Effects like reverb, delay, or wah-wah remove tonal definition and have also been suspected of pushing maximum speed beyond what a guitarist can cleanly play, according to Herbst's (2017c) study.

The notion of the superhuman has been prevalent in the virtuosity discourse. From a neoliberal perspective, guitar scholar George Turner (2015: 156) argues that virtuosic guitarists compete to gain an advantage in the marketplace. Likewise, performance researcher Daniel Leech-Wilkinson (2018) suggests that virtuosity has become a problem because excellence is now the norm, and every advance forces other musicians to follow suit. With global connectivity through the Internet, a state of competition has emerged that puts pressure on musicians to continuously improve their level of playing. Evidence of such pressure comes from guitar media reporting several scandals on Instagram and YouTube in late 2019, with virtuosos accused of faking their video-recorded performances. Similarly, Internet celebrity Jared Dines challenged Manuel Gardner Fernandes for speeding up a now-deleted video posted on Instagram, stating that 'hands don't glitch like that' (Astley-Brown, 2019b). Fernandes responded on his Instagram channel:

> I have indeed edited and pre-recorded some of my videos. Not because I'm unable to perform my ideas, but to give you the music in the best quality and to add an extra 2% of perfection to it. That being said, there was NEVER only one single video that has been sped up. I know some clips might look odd, but it really comes down to the fact that I'm recording just with my phone on auto mode. I have no other suggestion as to what caused the confusion here. I really hope that I haven't let anyone down and that some of you will still follow me on my journey as a musician. Me and my band are more than just motivated to make big things happen in the future and to get guitar-centred music in a better place on a broad scale. (Fernandes, 2019)

This statement illustrates that perfection is expected, and is one reason why musicians are followed in virtuosic guitar scenes. Guitarists appear to be caught in a paradox. They cannot merely publish a spontaneously produced, seemingly authentic video of their playing, yet neither can they afford to release anything less than perfect. If performances are perfect, guitarists must prove authenticity or be accused of cheating. In the progressive rock guitar scenes, performing virtuosity seems to be a constant requirement also for those who do not explicitly seek it. Success is inevitably tied to technical ability, even if musicians see themselves as artists and composers rather than virtuosic performers.

The cheating allegations against Fernandes triggered several responses to raise awareness of trickery and enable musicians to spot it. Jack Gardiner (2019a) [video] demonstrates the most common methods to speed up video performances in a half-hour-long video. These include recording solos note by note or phrase by phrase at a slower tempo and then speeding them up. Phrasings like vibrato and whammy bar appear more natural when parts of a real-tempo recording are edited into the sped-up performance. Furthermore, audio exports from Guitar Pro are run through a regular amplifier simulation plug-in in the digital audio workstation and enhanced with reverb to create a machine-perfect but entirely artificial performance. In some instances, the performed but sped-up performance is doubled by the artificial Guitar Pro performance, which is transposed up an octave to disguise the artifice. The video is either sped up too or recorded at the correct speed but with the sound replaced by the manufactured performance to avoid unnatural movements of hands, head, and hair.

Gardiner (2019a) [video] and others, like popular YouTubers Jared Dines (Astley-Brown, 2019a) and Leon Todd (2019) [video], see trickery as an ethical problem mainly for two reasons: it detracts from the accomplishments of players who do not cheat, and it raises the bar for speed and cleanliness to an unachievable level. This issue is widely discussed in *Guitar World* magazine (Astley-Brown, 2019a, 2019b, 2020a). Gardiner (2019a) argues that fake videos set unrealistic goals for aspiring players, negatively impacting mental health and potentially 'killing the future of this instrument for the next generation'. Gardiner (2019a) and Todd (2019) posit that beauty lies in imperfection, as heard in the guitar's characteristic string noise, variations in pick attack, and slightly off-pitch bendings. They concede that while perfect performances have aesthetic value and may be essential to the realisation of compositions, any touch-up must be made transparent out of fairness to other players. Such honesty would be required from highly technical performers as well as neo-soul players claiming to have composed and recorded a song in less than an hour, which is de facto meticulously produced. The same applies to the seemingly perfect improvisation that is entirely prepared. In such cases, besides the improvisational skills, the playing skills are misleading because technically executing demanding solos on the spot is more difficult than playing composed and rehearsed solos, as virtuoso Govan (2020a: 69) argues.

Lucas Mann of Rings of Saturn provides another example of how musicians deal with accusations of cheating, as reported in *Guitar World* (Bienstock, 2019b). To respond to claims of speeding up videos and using playbacks in live shows, Mann (2019) [video] released a 40-minute video explaining why neither accusation was true. He recorded a phrase accused of trickery into the digital audio workstation in real-time, evidenced by the clock in the software, to a click track without backing music. The amplifier signal and the guitar's direct output were recorded and uploaded for the critical viewer to assess. Further evidence of authentic live playing came from the band's audio engineer, playing recordings of several shows from the mixing console. At the core of the accusation is that faked live qualities help the band sell tickets. Mann stresses that toxic accusations on the Internet caused physical threats, career breaks due to mental health problems, and the loss of endorsement opportunities, highlighting how seriously perfection and authenticity are treated in the scene.

The tension between authenticity and perfection is nothing new in popular music. Singers have long been touched up with performance-enhancing processing, such as pitch correction, compression, equalisation and time and modulation effects (James, 2007; Provenzano, 2018). Live performances were sometimes entirely faked, as in the well-known case of Milli Vanilli (Espina & Sorenson, 2015). Drum performances have been quantised, and sounds enhanced or replaced, especially in metal music (Mynett, 2017). Fans have been critically appraising electric guitar playing for decades, if only to discuss their favourite virtuoso. Global connectivity and the popularity of video and social media platforms eventually created a competitive atmosphere fuelled by distrust, facilitated by the possibilities of deception through manipulating audio and video recordings, which is easily achieved with computer software. This hostile online environment is not unique to guitar culture; it is consistent with the 'shaming' culture within popular music and society more widely (Cheng, 2018; Ronson, 2015). Competitiveness and potential animosity are nevertheless more pronounced among guitarists than bassists and drummers, reviving the 1980s guitar competition, as per *Guitar World* (Astley-Brown, 2020a). The authenticity of technical prowess as a key component of the musician's integrity and commitment is under scrutiny in the virtuoso guitar communities, forcing guitarists to prove that their videos and live performances are not fake. Traditionalist authenticity in the Romantic tradition (Keightley, 2001; Moore, 2002; Waksman, 2003) is upheld in current scenes, notwithstanding modernistic ambitions of progress regarding higher speeds, greater cleanliness, and new adaptations of established techniques and technologies.

7 The Virtual Scene, and How Contemporary Virtuosos Make a Living

In contrast to the rock guitar heroes of the 1960s and 1970s, many virtuosos of the 1980s and 1990s did not receive mainstream attention. Unless they were in a commercial rock or metal band, most played to a niche audience. A few special-interest record labels (such as Shrapnel) helped them record and release their music, mostly in a DIY fashion with little promotion (Wiederhorn, 2015). Interaction among fans and between fans and artists took place face-to-face at concerts or music conventions, in print guitar magazines, on noticeboards, and through instructional videos (Walser, 1992: 299). Though international, the scene was not well connected. Fast-forward to the twenty-first century: forums such as *Ultimate Guitar* and message boards on the websites of players such as John Petrucci and Paul Gilbert have become the new, interactive way of communicating. Hosting a forum has, on occasion, led to contributions from known virtuosos to fan discussions, which was a rare but welcome highlight, especially since musicians from the 1970s were not accessible at all. Although social media emerged less than twenty years ago, its proliferation has significantly impacted the electric guitar scenes. MySpace lost relevance and Facebook conceded its primacy to Instagram and YouTube (Hyatt, 2016). Purely text-based communication has shifted to bite-sized videos and photos. Asynchronous interaction has increasingly become synchronous, with live performances and question-and-answer sessions allowing fans to interact directly with revered musicians.

In contemporary rock guitar scenes, many players have embraced social media as a strategy to offset shrinking budgets in the music industry (Fitterman Radbill, 2017; Weissman, 2017). Music industry experts John Williamson and Martin Cloonan (2013: 16) suggest that the industry's primary income source has shifted from record sales to live music, with its associated opportunities to sell merchandise and records without a label or distributor. This assessment is consistent with most music business manuals, some of which claim that 90 to 95 per cent of an artist's income now stems from touring (Owsinski, 2016: 147–8). Yet touring poses its own problem, as it requires a large enough following to make it financially viable. Many rock and metal bands and artists playing guitar-led music struggle to break even. Even established acts suffer losses from touring, as Periphery guitarist Misha Mansoor reveals: 'we'll gross a fair bit but we won't net a lot. We did a five-week tour in Europe last year, we walked away with nothing' (Kennelty, 2018).

Dick Weissman (2017: 50) and Bobby Owsinski (2016: 217–8) suggest that social media has overturned the traditional model of success. A newly formed band typically begins by home recording and self-releasing an EP, playing local gigs, and forming a regional fan base on social media. Videos posted on YouTube are shared online, attracting attention and leading fans to websites that sell music without a label. A label that finances the production of a full debut album may eventually be found. Alternatively, the band may start their own label or release through another band's label (Owsinski, 2016: 217–8). Even without a label, music can be made available on major streaming services and via aggregator platforms at little cost. Many artists, such as solo guitarists Plini and Jason Richardson, have self-released their records. Sarah Longfield and Covet have released their music through independent niche labels with only a handful of releases per year. The closest equivalent to the influential Shrapnel label of the 1980s is Sumerian Records, where Periphery (Misha Mansoor), Animals as Leaders (Tosin Abasi), Born of Osiris (Jason Richardson), and Nita Strauss are signed. Regardless of the type of label, music is usually written, recorded, mixed, and produced in the artist's home studio or created through remote collaboration.

Through the Internet, the contemporary independent artist has various alternatives for distributing and selling without a record label, which also facilitates monetising a personality or performance style rather than the product. YouTube allows anyone to start a music career; a band is not required (Werner, 2017). Some current guitarists highlighted in greatest lists (see Section 2) have been in the spotlight for years without releasing a full-length album. Ichika Nito and Mateus Asato are two such players, best known for their videos posted on YouTube and promoted via Instagram. *Guitar World* describes Asato as a social media master who consistently posts 'short, engrossing videos displaying his dazzling technique in a variety of styles, from funk to fingerpicking to full-on shred' (Bienstock, 2019c), earning him public performances with American Idol star Tori Kelly, singer-songwriter Jessie J, and soul singer Bruno Mars. By contrast, Nito presents his music solely on YouTube, posting videos of himself alone or with other musicians in the scene. His collaborative video with Polyphia's Tim Henson received almost two million views within its first six months (Henson, 2020b) [video]. Especially popular are competition videos that involve recording a solo over the backing track of another artist or to the same backing track (Dines, 2019) [video], joint performances of a song by one of the artists (Nito, 2020a) [video], or series such as 'Shred Wars' (Dines, 2018b) [video] and other collaborations hosted by Jared Dines, some of which have more than eight million YouTube streams (Dines, 2018a) [video]. Most of Nito and Asato's videos are less than one minute long. Occasionally, a short Instagram video is available in a longer version on YouTube. These videos usually contain playing without a backing track, recorded in the performer's living room or bedroom, often with just a computer microphone. There is little or no talking; the only communication is one- or two-sentence descriptions (Asato, 2020a) [video]. The videos are probably kept short so that they are easy to follow and can be posted almost daily, as tends to be the case with Nito (e.g., Nito, 2020b [video]). Instead of full songs, they contain short cover versions or performances 'in the style of' (Asato, 2020a) [video] or nostalgic memories of the past, either of a particular guitarist (Asato, 2020c) [video] or the guitar scene. For example, Eddie Van Halen's passing in 2020 gave rise to many reminiscence videos (e. g. Burrell, 2020) [video]. Other artists, such as Sophie Lloyd, build their fan base by covering full-length pop and rock songs, usually in a shred style, combined with advertising signature gear (Lloyd, 2020b) [video] or paid educational content (Lloyd, 2020a) [video]. Some videos are dedicated to signature equipment and show the joy of design-ing and using them, demonstrating the celebrity's 'human' side, which makes them likeable (Asato, 2020b [video]; see also Click, Lee, & Holladay, 2013). Other social media-embracing virtuosos such as Yvette Young post videos of songs in the making (Young, 2020) [video]; Sarah Longfield shares videos of her preparations for masterclasses and other lessons (Longfield, 2020) [video]. Videos are occasionally posted with players reflecting on their weaknesses, as this description of a video by Mateus Asato shows:

> [T]his is for my guitar fellas: after 6 years of constantly posting 15 sec/60 sec guitar pieces on Instagram, I've realized that my sense of improvising got so much weaker. Well . . . honestly this was never 'a thing' in my playing, since the fact that I never got deep enough into blues & jazz roots & some other reasons. I understand that the way of seeing guitar as an instrument has been changing a lot lately – to the new generation of virtuosos, writing riffs/parts + play solos as clean as possible has become a major priority – and it seems that the concept of 'jamming' isn't the same comparing to the 80's/90's era . . . Anyway. This video is just a reminder to myself that sometimes you just have to press 'rec' and play, no matter how bad you and your ideas could sound. (Asato, 2019)

This video depicts another way of dealing with the pressure perfection causes (see also Cheng, 2018); rather than giving evidence of flawless technique, musicians join the ranks of other guitarists learning the instrument and making progress by working on their weaknesses. Additionally, many current players willingly give personal insights into their music in progress from their living room, creating a sense of intimacy (Ellcessor, 2012: 47). Being relatable, almost like a close friend (Baym, 2012), increases and sustains the fan base of artists, many of whom rarely perform live. Social media requires an emotional connec-tion to ensure followers remain engaged and buy products (Hyatt, 2016: 216), and a friend-like relationship helps achieve that (Click et al., 2013). According to the '1,000 true fans theory' (Kelly, 2008), only a relatively small number of dedicated followers is necessary for artists to make a living (see also Jin, 2020). Behind-the-scenes stories, insights into work in the making, interviews, and trivia (Owsinski, 2016: 219–23) connect with the 'tribe' (Godin, 2008), as can be observed on guitar virtuosos' social media channels.

Other concepts for building a personal relationship with an audience include letting the audience vote on the development of an artist's music; asking for recommendations on Instagram; and hosting impromptu Q&A sessions, tutorial videos, and contests (see also Bennett, 2016). One of the most effective approaches is live-streaming on Instagram, which allows artists to discuss topics of interest with their fan base or with each other and interact with their followers by responding to comments (e.g., Plini, 2020b). Some artists have discovered the potential of the video platform Twitch, where they can stream live guitar play-throughs with high-quality audio, including entire virtual concerts. Besides music-related streaming, the human side of these artists is shown in gaming streams, for which Twitch was initially created. During these sessions, artists can respond to the fans' comments in the chat. To monetise this activity further, followers can subscribe to the artist's Twitch channel, which gives them certain privileges, such as custom emojis, along with an icon next to their name in the chat, making it easier for the streamer to notice their comment. These subscriptions usually cost $5.00, of which Twitch takes 50 per cent, leaving the streamer with $2.50 per subscription (Brave, 2020). The streamer might also welcome donations with an attached message, usually read out publicly or displayed on the screen. This practice allows direct contact with an individual member of the fanbase, which may encourage others to donate in expectation of a personal response. There is no upper limit, but sometimes a minimum amount is asked for the donation message to appear onscreen. Notable Twitch-using guitarists are Herman Li, Tim Henson, Jason Richardson, and Matt Heafy. Altogether, whether for economic reasons or due to sincere interest, the contemporary artist interacts personally with their followers, thereby creating a real or imagined bond (Click et al., 2013; see also Marwick & Boyd, 2011). Whereas the aloof guitar hero was prevalent in the 1960s and 1970s, and the sympathetic but distant guitar god in the 1980s (Millard, 2004a, 2004b; Weinstein, 2013), guitar celebrities of the 2010s and 2020s maintain close and regular contact with their fans (see also Baym, 2012).

Social media seems mostly to be used either for attracting visitors to YouTube channels or for promoting products around music-making. Instagram guitarists such as Ichika Nito, Mateus Asato, Sophie Lloyd, and Sophie Burrell post easy-to-follow, short videos to market lessons and other services. Other artists, such as Plini and Aaron Marshall of Intervals, do not regularly post performance videos. Instead, they create public promotional material for their music, tours, and endorsement products. Both approaches are fruitful, and most artists fall somewhere in between. Few can afford to neglect social media altogether. Also, guitarists known for their social media work must release some music to lend legitimacy to their persona and allow them to offer more products. However, social media is a time-consuming business that takes away space for creative work. This is why Mateus Asato, who made his career through Instagram with a following of more than one million, closed his account in February 2021. He justified his decision in a *Guitar World* interview, noting the pressure of having to post high-quality content on social media almost daily at the cost of musical inspiration:

> Instagram is a place where I will be forever thankful in terms of my career . . . but I'm sincerely overwhelmed. This is such a great source of promoting your art but the more I spend time here the more I guess if we [are] still on the right path of why we make music. Instagram helped musicians to get better at business, at making flawless-performance videos (after uncountable takes). I got lost inside the boxes of the 15s–60s videos. I have a big feeling that we are loosing [sic] the essence of musicianship interaction. (Asato, in Roche 2021)

Asato's decision to exit social media to regain his passion for guitar playing has been supported by fellow guitarist Jack Gardiner (2021) [video], suggesting that social media competes with music-making, regardless of the opportunity it provides to make a living from music. Due to Instagram's format of short videos, playing is reduced to showcasing multiple virtuosic techniques with unnatural frequency and performing over four-bar chord progressions instead of developing musical phrases dynamically and naturally across several sections (Gardiner, 2021). Asato and Gardiner agree that such essentially 'unmusical' videos are no substitute for live interaction with other musicians. Constantly streaming brief but perfect snapshots causes pressure, as well as limiting practice time, so that such videos are hardly feasible in the long run.

Streaming is widely blamed for the decline of the music industry and the low royalties paid to artists and songwriters (Weissman, 2017: 68). In 2020, *The Sunday Times* reported that from co-writing a song for Kylie Minogue's 2020 album *Disco* (Sanderson, 2020), songwriter Fiona Bevan earned a meagre £100 in streaming royalties. If streaming proves unprofitable for songwriters in mainstream pop music, it is even worse for musicians in progressive niche genres.

Royalties vary on a case-by-case basis, but on average the popular streaming service Spotify paid $0.00318 per play/stream to artists in 2019 (Hearn, 2017; see also Pastukhov, 2019), and YouTube views paid out about half this sum: $0.00185 (Geyser, 2020). However, the quantity compensates for this.

According to Mark Halloran and Edward Hearn (2017: 78), YouTube is potentially more influential and impactful than any record label, radio, or television show. An overview of record release numbers, Spotify streams, and YouTube views (Table 7) demonstrates that business models vary between the different generations of rock guitar virtuosos.

Apart from Tom Morello, John Petrucci, and Zakk Wylde, who are not primarily solo artists, other virtuosos of the older generation have released more solo albums due to their decades-long careers. In contrast, current guitarists no longer focus on the album format. Gardiner (2019b) [audio] argues that EPs are preferred to full albums because the contemporary audiences' attention span does not last for a full album, especially for a debut release. Besides, EPs and singles have become a 'sideline' for many guitarists. Hence, the number of Spotify followers and monthly streams varies significantly between players, ranging from Sophie Lloyd (who more or less ignores music streaming) among the lowest to Joe Satriani and Tom Morello among the highest. YouTube and Instagram metrics are more balanced and vary between players and platforms, showing the relevance that individual guitarists attach to specific social media channels. Several newcomer guitarists in their twenties and early thirties with much shorter careers, such as Ichika Nito, Sophie Lloyd, and Mateus Asato, have as many or more YouTube views as longer-established virtuosos.

Income from royalties can only be estimated but prioritising YouTube over traditional record releases seems favourable, given the high number of streams and views at the previously mentioned royalty rates. In terms of streaming royalties, older generation guitarists can expect monthly revenues of between $1,900 (Joe Satriani) and $100 (Michael Angelo Batio), while the range for younger artists is between $800 (Plini) and $40 (Sarah Longfield). YouTube streaming income for older guitarists similarly ranges from $1,950 (Steve Vai) to $120 (Greg Howe). The top earner on YouTube is Ichika Nito. His estimated monthly income is $13,500, from a channel that has existed for only 24 months, with the prospect of increased views in the future. Considerable monthly earnings are also accrued by Sophie Lloyd ($2,800), Mateus Asato ($2,600), and Kiko Loureiro ($1,600). Other income streams, such as physical record sales and revenue from live shows, were not considered. New business models allow contemporary guitarists to have professional careers built on an entirely different musical practice: one that does not require playing in a band, recording in a studio, releasing records, or performing live. This assessment is consistent with a recent interview statement by Spotify CEO Daniel Ek, in which he suggests that the old business model of releasing records every few years is no longer working. Careers depend on social media activity:

Table 7 Record releases, Spotify streams, and YouTube views

Player	Solo discography	Spotify followers	Monthly Spotify streams	YouTube followers	Monthly YouTube plays	Instagram followers
			Current generation			
Asato, Mateus	5 singles	31 k	45 k	478 k	1,410 k	1,100 k
Lloyd, Sophie	1 EP	8 k	5 k	535 k	1,530 k	349 k
Longfield, Sarah	3 albums, 6 EPs	18 k	13 k	243 k	105 k	138 k
Loureiro, Kiko	5 albums	67 k	51 k	502 k	840 k	542 k
Nito, Ichika	7 EP	58 k	71 k	764 k	7,320 k	404 k
Mansoor, Misha	1 album	3 k	9 k	79 k	40 k	196 k
Plini	2 albums, 6 EPs	192 k	256 k	181 k	800 k	300 k
Richardson, Jason	1 album	37 k	57 k	93 k	210 k	202 k
Strauss, Nita	1 album	22 k	13 k	55 k	41 k	530 k
Young, Yvette	4 EPs	60 k	83 k	193 k	300 k	342 k

		Older generation				
Batio, Michael Angelo	14 albums	42 k	29 k	69 k	200 k	108 k
Gilbert, Paul	16 albums, 2 EPs	116 k	66 k	136 k	525 k	464 k
Howe, Greg	16 albums	42 k	50 k	40 k	66 k	85 k
Kotzen, Richie	22 albums, 1 EP	109 k	160 k	83 k	210 k	153 k
Malmsteen, Yngwie	21 albums, 2 EPs	274 k	345 k	65 k	200 k	297 k
Morello, Tom	2 solo albums	87 k	1,000 k	53 k	210 k	1,300 k
Petrucci, John	2 solo albums	116 k	164 k	55 k	270 k	630 k
Satriani, Joe	17 albums	450 k	603 k	372 k	240 k	647 k
Vai, Steve	9 albums, 2 EPs	368 k	388 k	537 k	1,050 k	846 k
Wylde, Zakk	3 solo albums	367 k	303 k	371 k	225 k	1,000 k

Note: Data from Spotify, YouTube, and Instagram; November 2020

> There is a narrative fallacy here, combined with the fact that, obviously, some artists that used to do well in the past may not do well in this future landscape, where you can't record music once every three to four years and think that's going to be enough. The artists today that are making it realise that it's about creating a continuous engagement with their fans. It is about putting the work in, about the storytelling around the album, and about keeping a continuous dialogue with your fans. I feel, really, that the ones that aren't doing well in streaming are predominantly people who want to release music the way it used to be released. (Ek, in *Music Ally*, 2020)

The new generation of artists often chooses middle-ground platforms like Bandcamp, where individual songs and entire albums can be sold for a fee of 10 to 15 per cent of the sale proceeds, plus payment processing charges (Bandcamp, 2021). Jack Gardiner's latest EP *Escapades* (Gardiner, 2020b) [audio] has had 173,050 streams on Spotify at the time of writing, for which he can expect royalties of approximately $550. By contrast, fewer than 100 sales of the EP on Bandcamp for $7.00 would have generated the same revenue (Gardiner, 2020a). Hence, it is in the interests of aspiring artists who focus on original music to direct their marketing efforts towards Bandcamp rather than the dominant streaming outlets.

In his survival guide for making music in the Internet age, Bobby Owsinski (2016) argues that contemporary artists must leverage various income streams due to the decline of traditional business models. Social media and YouTube seem to be the most promising platforms, not only because of the direct effect on artists' revenue but also as a marketing platform for other offerings (Hyatt, 2016). Traditional publishers discovered guitar tablature books in the 1980s as a source of revenue in the printed music market (Weissman, 2017: 143). Contemporary guitarists have adopted this strategy, selling tablature direct to their fans via their websites. Some of the most successful media masters, such as Ichika Nito, sell tablature plus supporting tutorial videos (Nito, 2021) [video]. Many current solo artists and bands such as Intervals, Plini, and Sithu Aye offer authorised tablature on the platform Sheet Happens (Sheet Happens, 2020) alongside other merchandise, including T-shirts, guitar picks, notepads, baseball caps, and face masks. Other artists, like Vitalism, Dan James Griffins, Ichika Nito, and Jason Richardson, prefer personal websites or Bandcamp profiles to avoid paying fees and to pocket more profit from selling tablature. Sophie Lloyd is among the players generating additional income through signature jewellery such as bracelets, necklaces, and earrings made from guitar strings sold on the platform Guitarwrist (2021).

Teaching and other forms of demonstration formed a major income stream for rock guitar virtuosos in the 1980s and 1990s, and continues to do so for the current generation. Contemporary guitarists perform at music conventions, deliver clinics in music stores, and give masterclasses online or as part of events hosted by established virtuosos. For example, in 2021 John Petrucci's four-day *Guitar Universe* featured Tosin Abasi, Mateus Asato, Kiko Loureiro, Plini, Jason Richardson, and Tom Quayle (Petrucci, 2020). Some virtuosos also offer individual lessons via video call applications or teach in person – for example, Yvette Young, Javier Reyes, Jack Gardiner, Tom Quayle, Josh Martin, Sophie Burrell, and Jason Richardson. For most contemporary virtuosos, lessons are a regular supplement to their income. Synchronous online video lessons may not be compatible with artists' schedules or too expensive for their fans, so many offer packaged video lessons that are more affordable and can be downloaded from their websites. For instance, Tom Quayle (2020b) sells a wide array of standardised, downloadable video- and score-based lessons, as do others such as Jack Gardiner, Jason Richardson, and Rick Graham. Another option is providing access to guitar courses and learning material from the artist through monthly paid subscriptions to a website, of which Ross Campbell's *Bulletproof Guitar Player* (2021) is an example. Others use the website Patreon, which allows artists to receive direct monthly financial support from their fans. Among its users are Sophie Burrell, Dan James Griffin, and Sithu Aye. Griffin and Aye utilise Patreon to distribute educational material, as well as to cultivate a deeper personal connection by allowing early access to their music and videos. Several artists, including Tom Quayle, Rick Graham, Jack Gardiner, and Sophie Lloyd, use YouTube for streaming sample educational content that advertises their standardised lesson bundles (e.g., Lloyd, 2020c) [video]. Those guitarists who do not focus on promoting their music and personality on social media generally tend to rely on teaching.

Live performances generate income for musicians too, especially when playing in popular bands such as Animals as Leaders, Polyphia, Periphery, Covet, Intervals, and Rings of Saturn. These musicians commonly play in medium to large clubs and at music festivals, but rarely as headliners or on the main stage unless booked by niche festivals for their particular genre of music.

Equipment is another source of income. With Abasi Concepts, Tosin Abasi offers instruments inspired by the contemporary electric guitar sound with a non-traditional approach to body shape. Misha Mansoor and former Periphery bassist and engineer Adam 'Nolly' Getgood founded GetGood Drums to sell drum sample libraries. Many contemporary virtuosos, like earlier players, endorse a brand, sometimes with their own signature series (Table 8). As sociologist Deena Weinstein notes, 'Guitar gods are not only players; they also serve to merchandize equipment, whether or not they are paid shills. They are the link between the product and the manufacturers' profit' (Weinstein, 2013: 148).

Table 8 Signature equipment

Player	Instruments	Amplifiers	Effects	Other
		Current generation		
Abasi, Tosin	Abasi Concepts, Ibanez	Neural DSP plug-in		DiMarzio and Fishman pickups
Asato, Mateus	Suhr		Jackson Audio	Suhr pickups
Gates, Synyster	Schecter			Seymour Duncan
Lloyd, Sophie	Kiesel			
Longfield, Sarah	Strandberg			
Loureiro, Kiko	Ibanez		Zoom	
Nito, Ichika	Ibanez			
Mansoor, Misha	Jackson	Peavey, Toneforge plug-in		BKP pickups
Plini	Strandberg	Neural DSP plug-in		
Richardson, Jason	Music Man	Toneforge plug-in		
Strauss, Nita	Ibanez			DiMarzio pickups
Young, Yvette	Ibanez			

Older generation

Batio, Michael Angelo	Sawtooth, Dean		T-Rex	ChromaCast string dampener
Gilbert, Paul	Ibanez		JHS Pedals	
Howe, Greg	Kiesel, Laguna, Carvin	DV Mark	Carl Martin	
Kotzen, Richie	Fender	Victory	Tech 21, Zoom	DiMarzio pickups
Malmsteen, Yngwie	Fender	Marshall	Fender	Seymour Duncan pickups
Morello, Tom	Fender		Dunlop	
Petrucci, John	Music Man	Mesa Boogie	TC Electronics, Dunlop	DiMarzio pickups
Satriani, Joe	Ibanez	Marshall, Peavey	Vox	DiMarzio & Sustainiac pickups
Vai, Steve	Ibanez	Synergy	Morley, Eventide	DiMarzio pickups
Wylde, Zakk	Gibson, Dean, Wylde Audio	Marshall	MXR	EMG pickups, EV speakers

Signature equipment is equally given to current artists, evidencing how successful contemporary social media-focused business models are. Some receive items either from big instrument manufacturers such as Ibanez, or from smaller companies that specialise in extended-range guitars and cater to contemporary artists' needs. That artists' focus on the instrument, pickups, and amplifier plug-ins rather than on hardware amplifiers and effects is understandable, given that the stage of contemporary guitarists is more often the Internet than the arena.

Endorsements are more easy to obtain than signature equipment. This involves artists being granted discounted gear under mutually beneficial marketing expectations. Dan James Griffin has disclosed the terms of his endorsement with the guitar company Strandberg:

> When I was with Strandberg my requirements were to post a video/photo once a week with the product, grow my social media presence by 20% within the first year, and then another 30% within the second (a total of 50%), and finally perform 8 times a year minimum. All in all, this was pretty achievable! The only difficult one was growing my following by 50%, but with the help of Strandberg also promoting me this came by pretty quickly. (Griffin, 2020)

While Strandberg emphasise social media, more established companies, such as string manufacturer D'Addario, may ask their endorsed artists to perform at events like guitar shows, Griffin further explains. Due to the exclusivity of larger manufacturers, smaller brands such as Strandberg, Ormsby, and Aristides are more attractive to guitarists at the beginning of their careers. Apart from discounted or free gear, endorsements help promising artists receive publicity from a larger following.

Close relationships with a brand may open further opportunities for artists, such as developing signature gear. Guitarists do not receive royalties or profits from sales of already-existing gear. When it comes to signature gear and big companies, Tosin Abasi shared his experience with Ibanez:

> I was an Ibanez guy for a long time, and often with Ibanez, they have existing models and maybe they let you paint it a certain color you like or put some signature pickups . . . They were open for that, which was really cool. I dug being on Ibanez because they were always open to pushing the guitar forward, so they let me begin working on my own unique shape, and they agreed to multiscale and had these ergonomic ideas and they were all down for that . . . But it took, like, multiple years because an operation of that size, it takes time. (Abasi, in Jomatami, 2020)

Abasi founded his brand, Abasi Concepts, to design guitars to his liking due to slow manufacture and design constraints, pointing to the downside of signature gear from big manufacturers. It is likely for similar reasons that John Petrucci abandoned Ibanez for smaller Earnie Ball/Music Man, Zakk Wylde left Gibson to start his own brand Wylde Audio in collaboration with Schecter, and Eddie Van Halen moved the popular 5150 amplifier model from Peavey to his EVH brand, which also offers his EVH Wolfgang guitars.

Recently, more female players have gained prominence at a professional level in guitar communities, as is reflected in increased musical instrument sponsorships. Yvette Young, Nita Strauss, and Sarah Longfield are amongst the best known to have received signature instruments. Ibanez endorser Lari Basilio is another guitarist influential in contemporary guitar scenes. Sophie Burrell has a large Instagram following for her original music, and is sponsored by Paul Reed Smith guitars. Strandberg-endorsed emerging guitarist Soumia Ghechami has gained traction on social media with her releases of covers and short original video clips, much like YouTube expert Mateus Asato. Carolyn Barba is artist making waves on Instagram, endorsed by Fishman Music.

8 Conclusion

Popular music has changed significantly from the rock music of the 1960s and 1970s to encompass entirely new genres, many of which involve few or no physical instruments. Throughout this development, the electric guitar has not changed fundamentally, yet the design of and approach to the instrument, including its surrounding culture, have evolved considerably. The 1960s and 1970s saw the rise of the rock guitar hero as a result of technological innovation and the cultural zeitgeist (Millard, 2004a; Weinstein, 2013). In the 1980s, the guitar hero became the guitar god through rock and metal spectacles (Millard, 2004b). However, not all guitarists of the time enjoyed mainstream success. From the heyday of shred, many of those included in lists of greatest guitar players of all time, genre, or era are known only to guitarists interested in progressive guitar music. In this respect, little has changed. Contemporary virtuosos are featured in guitar media, more often online than in print. Many enjoy a large following, primarily online among fellow guitarists, but only some appear in the mainstream. Nita Strauss is the live guitarist for the Alice Cooper band, and Tosin Abasi has written arrangements for Ariana Grande and is a judge on the US-American 'No Cover' contest show alongside Alice Cooper and Lzzy Hale. Various websites suggest that Polyphia have broken into the mainstream with their electronic and hip-hop-inspired sound (e.g., Academy Music Group, 2019). Another movement into mainstream rock was the first-ever instrumental act at the Download Festival in 2018, Plini [video]. More recently, pop star Doja Cat performed a rock version of her track 'Say So' (Doja Cat, 2020) at the 2020 MTV European Music Awards [video], for which the musical director opted to copy a riff from Plini's track 'Handmade Cities' (Plini, 2016) [audio].

These ventures into the mainstream, which tend not to compromise the music's progressive nature, should not obscure the fact that many contemporary virtuosos are independent artists exploring guitar playing and writing progressive rock music with little commercial consideration. Fans value their novelty, creativity, and playing technique. In a modernist tradition, a virtuoso's appeal requires constant novelty, achieved mainly through the ever-faster mastery of a growing repertoire of standard licks with small expansions of technique. That is consistent with the history of popular music, where novelty has always been built on the old and has been gradual rather than sudden and substantial (Dale, 2016). Progress is achieved through a pattern of 'novelty, ossification, stagnation, new novelty' while acknowledging earlier achievements (Dale, 2016: 85). This pattern is reflected in the world of rock guitar virtuosos; artists pay tribute to and build on their forerunners.

Progressive rock guitarists have expanded their skill sets. The contemporary virtuoso commands a wide range of solo techniques and, like many first-generation rock guitar heroes, pays attention to rhythm, expressive tone, and technology. They may require broader skills beyond playing the instrument than in the past. Guitarists write, arrange, record, and produce their music in a DIY manner, often adding extra elements such as electronic beats, live electronics, and other forms of contemporary sound design. They create artwork and animated videos for their songs. They run websites and sell their music, tablature, lessons, and merchandise on other platforms. They regularly produce videos for their social media channels. What once was delegated to labels, managers, or other support staff is now carried out by artists themselves. They have become 'cultural entrepreneurs' (Morris, 2014), defined by the 'hyphen' (Fitterman Radbill, 2017: 63): virtuoso-guitarist-composer-innovator-producer-promoter-YouTuber-teacher-entrepreneur.

The increasing affordability of music technology and the opportunities provided by Web 2.0 have democratised music-making in numerous ways. Traditional hierarchies of power appear to have been dismantled so that musicians from different backgrounds and nationalities could become professionals, contributing to more diverse virtuoso rock guitar communities. Many accomplished players have backgrounds in Africa, South America, Asia, and Australia. Gender is a different matter, with inequality still apparent. Where, Deena Weinstein asks, where 'are all the guitar goddesses, the guitar heroines, the guitar virtuosas?' (Weinstein, 2013: 151). Guitarist and scholar John Strohm quotes Blake Babies' lead guitarist Juliana Hatfield: 'how many women are there who have actually been innovative, technically accomplished lead guitarists? None! There aren't any. All of the great, original, innovative electric guitarists have been men' (Strohm, 2004: 182). However, this is only a half-truth: women have made names for themselves as exceptional guitar players since the advent of the electric guitar, from Sister Rosetta Tharpe to The Great Kat to Lita Ford to Jennifer Batten. The problem has rarely been that women were not trusted to play like men, but they were not welcome in the scene. At least virtuoso guitar communities give indications of gradual change. Inventive players such as Yvette Young, Sarah Longfield, and Nita Strauss are regularly featured in guitar media and recognised as equals by their fellow musicians. Strauss became the first woman ever to receive a signature guitar from influential manufacturer Ibanez in 2017, and Young recently followed suit. Likewise, Longfield received her signature model with Strandberg Guitars, alongside other successful players like Plini. Women receiving signature gear and media coverage is a big step towards equality. However, full equality is still a long way off, given the imbalance in streaming numbers and lower popularity, as exemplified by YouTube and Spotify followers.

Electric guitar playing has come a long way and has always been a mirror for the development of culture and society over time, as has popular music in general (see Dale, 2016). Even though the guitar is still a traditional instrument in the sense that authentic connection between the fingers, instrument, and audience is valued, the pillars of success are originality and novelty in playing and inventive uses of technology. Romantic tradition-consciousness and modernistic striving for novelty characterise the scenes. This friction is perhaps what nurtures creativity in guitar-led rock music and drives the instrument's further development.

Appendix

Analysed Guitar Manuals Used for Canonical Analysis

Alexander, J. (2018). *The Complete Technique for Modern Guitar: Develop Perfect Guitar Technique and Master Picking, Legato, Rhythm and Expression*. Fundamental Changes.

Basener, C. (2011). *The Essential Guide to Alternate Picking: Improve Your Picking Technique and Develop Killer Chops for Precise Lead Playing*. CreateSpace.

Brooks, C. A. (2017). *Neo Classical Speed Strategies for Guitar: Master Speed Picking for Shred Guitar and Play Fast – The Yng Way!* Fundamental Changes.

Brooks, C. A. (2018a). *Legato Guitar Technique Mastery: Legato Technique Speed Mechanics, Licks and Sequences for Guitar*. Fundamental Changes.

Brooks, C. A. (2018b). *Sweep Picking Speed Strategies for Guitar: Essential Guitar Techniques, Arpeggios and Licks for Total Fretboard Mastery*. Fundamental Changes.

Brooks, C. A. (2019). *Sweep Picking Speed Strategies for 7-String Guitar: Discover Seven-String Guitar Arpeggios, Techniques and Licks*. Fundamental Changes.

Dillard, K. (2007). *Intelli-Shred: The Thinking Musician's Guide to Melodic Mastery*. Alfred.

George, A. (2018). *High Intensity Guitar Technique: Book 1. The Foundations of Proper Guitar Technique*. Independent.

George, A. (2019). *High Intensity Guitar Technique: Book 2. Professional Techniques*. Independent.

George, A. (2020). *High Intensity Guitar Technique: Book 3. Virtuoso Techniques*. Independent.

Govan, G. (2002a). *Creative Guitar: Advanced Techniques*. Sanctuary Publishing.

Govan, G. (2002b). *Creative Guitar: Cutting-Edge Techniques*. Sanctuary Publishing.

Harrison, G. (2009). *Shred Guitar: A Guide to Extreme Rock and Metal Lead Techniques*. Hal Leonard.

Herman, L. (2012). *Advanced Guitar Theory and Technique Applied to the Metal and Shred Genres*. CreateSpace Independent Publishing.

Herman, L. (2014). *Advanced Guitar Diatonic Exercises to Build Speed and Technique for the Shred Metal Guitarist*. CreateSpace Independent Publishing.

Martone, D. (2012). *Serious Shred: Advanced Scales*. Alfred.

Meeker, J. (2012). *Serious Shred: Essential Concepts*. Alfred.

Neyens, K. (2020). *Creative Tapping for Modern Guitar: Discover Creative Guitar Tapping Techniques and Licks for Any Musical Genre*. Fundamental Changes.

Reyes, A. A. (2020). *Neoclassical Shred Guitar*. Amazon.

Riley, G. (2004). *Progressive Rock Guitar: A Guitarist's Guide to the Styles and Techniques of Art Rock*. Alfred.

Riley, G. (2012). *Serious Shred: Essential Techniques*. Alfred.

Schauss, G. (2012). *The Total Shred Guitarist: A Fun and Comprehensive Overview of Shred Guitar Playing*. Alfred.

Schauss, G. (2017). *Speed Guitar: Learn Lightning Fast Alternate Picking and Coordination*. Alfred.

Stetina, T. (1990). *Speed Mechanics for Lead Guitar*. Hal Leonard.

Stump, J. (2014). *Metal Guitar Chop Shop: Building Shred and Metal Technique*. Berklee Press.

Stump, J. (2017). *Guitar Sweep Picking and Arpeggios*. Berklee Press.

Syrek, T. (2000). *Shred is Not Dead: Concepts and Techniques for the Aspiring Rock Lead Guitar Virtuoso*. Alfred.

Thorpe, R. (2016). *Progressive Metal Guitar: An Advanced Guide to Modern Metal Guitar*. Fundamental Changes.

Thorpe, R. (2019). *Heavy Metal Lead Guitar: An Introduction to Heavy Metal Soloing for Guitar*. Fundamental Changes.

Zoupa, C. (2018). *Ultimate Shred Machine: The Ultimate Guide to Picking, Tapping and Sweeping*. Fundamental Changes.

Greatest Guitarists Lists Used for Canonical Analysis
Greatest and Most Influential Guitar Players

Bitoun, J. (2018). *Guitars and Heroes: Mythic Guitars and Legendary Musicians*. Firefly Books.

Editor Choice (2020). The Greatest Guitarists of All Time. *Editor Choice*. www.editorchoice.com/the-greatest-guitarists-of-all-time-ranked.

Kitts, J. & Tolinski, B. (2002). *Guitar World Presents the 100 Greatest Guitarists of All Time!* Hal Leonard.

Louder (2018). The 50 Best Guitarists of All Time. *Louder*. www.loudersound .com/features/the-50-greatest-guitarists-of-all-time.

Loudwire (2016). The 66 Best Hard Rock and Metal Guitarists of All Time. *Loudwire*. https://loudwire.com/top-hard-rock-metal-guitarists-of-all-time.

Ranker (2020). The Greatest Guitarists of All Time. *Ranker*. www.ranker.com/crowdranked-list/the-greatest-guitarists-of-all-time.

Rankings (2020). Top Ten Greatest Guitarists of All Time. *Rankings*. www.rankings.com/music-guitar-legends (originally accessed 18 Feb. 2021; no longer accessible at time of publication).

Rensen, M. & Stösser, V. (2011). *Guitar Heroes*. PPV Medien.

Rolling Stone (2015). 100 Greatest Guitarists. *Rolling Stone*. www.rollingstone.com/music/music-lists/100-greatest-guitarists-153675/lindsey-buckingham-39147.

Rubin, D. (2018). *100 Great Guitarists and the Gear That Made Them Famous*. Hal Leonard.

Sulem, M. (2020). Guitar Gods: The 30 Most Influential Lead Guitarists of All Time. *Yard Barker*. www.yardbarker.com/entertainment/articles/guitar_gods_the_30_most_influential_lead_guitarists_of_all_time (originally accessed 18 Feb. 2021; no longer accessible at time of publication).

The Mystique (2019). The 25 Best Rock Guitarists of All-Time. *The Mystique*. Retrieved from www.themystique.com/music/the-25-best-rock-guitarists-of-all-time.

Total Guitar (2020). The 100 Greatest Guitarists of All Time. *Total Guitar*. www.guitarworld.com/features/the-100-greatest-guitarists-of-all-time/1.

Turner, D. & Rubin, D. (2020). The 12 Most Influential Guitarists of All Time. *Guitar Player*. www.guitarplayer.com/players/the-12-most-influential-guitarists-of-all-timeand-their-signature-styles.

Vintage Guitar (2018). Top 100 Guitarists. *Vintage Guitar*. www.vintageguitar.com/25972/top-30-guitarists.

Greatest Metal Players

Entertainment (2020). 100 Greatest Heavy Metal Guitar Players from the 80s and 90s. *Entertainment*. https://entertainment.expertscolumn.com/100-greatest-heavy-metal-guitar-players-80s-and-90s.

Guitar Metrics (2020). Top 10 Heavy Metal Guitarists. *Guitar Metrics*. https://guitarmetrics.com/blogs/top-guitar-virtuosos-in-the-world/top-10-heavy-metal-guitarists (originally accessed 18 Feb. 2021; no longer accessible at time of publication).

Loudwire (2016). The 66 Best Hard Rock and Metal Guitarists of All Time. *Loudwire*. https://loudwire.com/top-hard-rock-metal-guitarists-of-all-time.

McIver, J. (2008). *The 100 Greatest Metal Guitarists*. London: Jawbone.

Total Guitar (2020). The 100 Greatest Guitarists of All Time. *Total Guitar*. www.guitarworld.com/features/the-100-greatest-guitarists-of-all-time/4.

Virtuosos and Shredders

All Music (2020). Guitar Virtuoso. *All Music*. www.allmusic.com/style/guitar-virtuoso-ma0000002630/artists.

Guitar Metrics (2019). Top Guitar Virtuosos of the World. *Guitar Metrics*. https://guitarmetrics.com/blogs/top-guitar-virtuosos-in-the-world/top-gui tar-virtuosos-in-the-world.

Guitar World (2015). Need for Speed: The 50 Fastest Shred Guitarists of All Time. *Guitar World*. www.guitarworld.com/magazine/50-fastest-guitarists-all-time.

McIver, J. (2008). *The 100 Greatest Metal Guitarists*. London: Jawbone.

Total Guitar (2020). The 100 Greatest Guitarists of All Time. *Total Guitar*. www.guitarworld.com/features/the-100-greatest-guitarists-of-all-time/5.

Newcomers and Notable Players of the Last Decade

Bienstock, R. (2019c). The 20 Best Guitarists of the Decade. *Guitar World*. www.guitarworld.com/artists/the-20-best-guitarists-of-the-decade.

Ear to The Ground Music (2020). 10 Best Guitarists of this Decade. *Ear to the Ground Music*. www.eartothegroundmusic.co/2020/07/27/10-best-guitarists-of-this-decade.

Guitar.com (2019). Meet the New Breed: 50 of the Most Exciting Young Guitarists in the World. *Guitar.Com*. https://guitar.com/guides/essential-guide/best-young-guitarists-in-the-world.

Sidwell, J. (2018). 10 Contemporary Guitar Virtuosos You Need to Hear. *Music Radar*. www.musicradar.com/news/10-contemporary-guitar-virtuosos-you-need-to-hear.

Total Guitar (2020). The 100 Greatest Guitarists of All Time. *Total Guitar*. www.guitarworld.com/features/the-100-greatest-guitarists-of-all-time/7.

Listening and Media Examples

This Element discusses numerous musical examples. Officially released music referred to is compiled in a Spotify playlist (titled: Cambridge Elements: Rock Guitar Virtuosos, https://open.spotify.com/playlist/0jp9v57PFFceDw5E20iQgr?si=mlR6O7-0SLGW0tk0FNP17A&nd=1). In cases where video examples are appropriate to demonstrate performance aspects, original video footage is provided in a YouTube playlist (titled: Cambridge Elements: Rock Guitar Virtuosos, www.youtube.com/watch?v=RLsEvZgmRVA&list=PLmnFgZLBYS7h81H-_L604gw6kUZtVkofZ). In both cases, direct links are given in the text to facilitate illustration.

References

Guitar manuals and greatest lists used for canonical analysis (Section 2) are listed in the Appendix to avoid duplication.

Primary Sources

Abasi Concepts (2020). Modern Solutions for the Modern Guitarist. https://abasiconcepts.com.

Abasi, T. (2020). Thump! *Guitar Messenger*. https://store.guitarmessenger.com/thump.

Academy Music Group (2019). An Interview With: Polyphia. *Academy Music Group*. https://academymusicgroup.com/blogs/interview-polyphia (originally accessed 18 Feb. 2021; no longer accessible at time of publication).

Altheide, D. & Schneider, C. (2013). *Qualitative Media Analysis*. Sage.

Anderson, E. R. & Zanetti, G. (2000). Comparative Semantic Approaches to the Idea of a Literary Canon. *The Journal of Aesthetics and Art Criticism*, **58**(4), 341–60.

Animals as Leaders (2011). An Infinite Regression. On *Weightless*. Prosthetic Records.

Animals as Leaders (2014a). Mind-Spun. On *The Joy of Motion*. Prosthetic Records.

Animals as Leaders (2014b). The Woven Web. On *The Joy of Motion*. Prosthetic Records.

Animals as Leaders (2016). Private Visions of The World. On *The Madness of Many*. Sumerian Records.

Appen, R. von & Doehring, A. (2006). Nevermind The Beatles, here's Exile 61 and Nico: 'The Top 100 Records of All Time'. *Popular Music*, **25**(1), 21–39.

Asato, M. (2019). Rec and Play. *Instagram*. www.instagram.com/tv/CAi4mS7j4RX.

Asato, M. (2020a). Dear Jimi. *YouTube*. www.youtube.com/watch?v=dZwiB6ao2w4.

Asato, M. (2020b). It's a Process. *Instagram*. www.instagram.com/tv/CDbsreAH11Q.

Asato, M. (2020c). Nostalgic Childhood. *YouTube*. www.youtube.com/watch?v=1f2yl3-KV2Q.

Astley-Brown, M. (2019a). Are Your Favorite Instagram Guitarists Faking their Incredible Technique? *Guitar World*. www.guitarworld.com/news/are-your-favorite-instagram-guitarists-actually-faking-it.

Astley-Brown, M. (2019b). Manuel Gardner Fernandes Responds to Instagram Fakery Accusations: 'There Was Never a Video that Was Sped Up'. *Guitar World*. www.guitarworld.com/news/manuel-gardner-fernandes-responds-to-instagram-fakery-accusations-there-was-never-a-video-that-was-sped-up.

Astley-Brown, M. (2019c). Polyphia vs Covet Round Table: 'I Hope that Guitar Music Dies. I Want it to Die a Painful Death'. *Music Radar*. www.musicradar.com/news/polyphia-vs-covet-round-table-i-hope-that-guitar-music-dies-i-want-it-to-die-a-painful-death.

Astley-Brown, M. (2020a). The Biggest Threat to the Guitar? It Could Well Be Guitarists: How Online Hate Endangers the Instrument We Love. *Guitar World*. www.guitarworld.com/features/the-biggest-threat-to-the-guitar-it-could-well-be-guitarists-how-online-hate-endangers-the-instrument-we-love.

Astley-Brown, M. (2020b). Polyphia's Tim Henson Demonstrates Jaw-Dropping 'God Hand' 8-String Slapping Riff. *Guitar World*. www.guitarworld.com/news/polyphias-tim-henson-demonstrates-jaw-dropping-god-hand-8-string-slapping-riff-and-teaches-you-how-to-play-it.

Bandcamp (2021). Getting Paid. https://bandcamp.com/pricing.

Batio, M. A. (1994). *No Boundaries*. M.A.C.E. Music.

Batio, M. A. (2003). *Speed Kills*. Vol. 1. Metal Method.

Batio, M. A. (2004). *Speed Kills*. Vol. 2. Metal Method.

Baym, N. (2012). Fans of Friends? Seeing Social Media Audiences as Musicians Do. *Participations: Journal of Audience and Reception Studies*, **9**(2), 286–316.

Beato, R. (2020). Tosin Abasi Talks Difference Between Prog & Progressive, Shares Opinion on Allan Holdsworth & Eddie Van Halen. www.ultimateguitar.com/news/general_music_news/tosin_abasi_talks_difference_between_prog__progressive_shares_opinion_on_allan_holdsworth__eddie_van_halen.html.

Becker, J. (1988a). Altitudes. On *Perpetual Burn*. Shrapnel.

Becker, J. (1988b). *Perpetual Burn*: Shrapnel.

Belladonna (2013). Van Halen Did Not Invent Tapping! This Italian Guy Did in 1965! *YouTube*. www.youtube.com/watch?v=d09pnxTSnT4.

Bennett, A. & Dawe, K. (eds.) (2001). *Guitar Cultures*. Berg.

Bennett, L. (2016). Singer-Songwriters in the Digital Age: New Trajectories in Connectivity and Participation Between Musicians and Fans on Social Media. In K. A. Williams and J. A. Williams (eds.), *The Cambridge Companion to the Singer-Songwriter*. Cambridge University Press, 329–40.

Bestguitarvids (2011). Scott Mishoe Slapping on the Guitar and Demonstrating some Nice Arpeggios. *YouTube*. www.youtube.com/watch?v=Tw2cQ94X cgI&ab_channel=bestguitarvids.

Bienstock, R. (2019a). Jason Richardson: 'I Was a High-School Kid Watching John Petrucci Play his Music Man . . . Now I Have my own Signature Model'. *Guitar World*. www.guitarworld.com/artists/jason-richardson-i-was-a-high-school-kid-watching-john-petrucci-play-his-music-man-now-i-have-my-own-signature-model.

Bienstock, R. (2019b). Rings of Saturn's Lucas Mann Responds to Allegations he 'Mimed' Guitar Parts Onstage. *Guitar World*. www.guitarworld.com/news/rings-of-saturns-lucas-mann-responds-to-allegations-he-mimed-gui tar-parts-onstage.

Bienstock, R. (2020). Al Joseph: 'It's Easy to Learn Techniques – It's Harder to Make the Guitar Sing'. *Guitar World*. www.guitarworld.com/features/al-joseph-its-easy-to-learn-techniques-its-harder-to-make-the-guitar-sing? fbclid=IwAR1WTi4MS-Ma5OKWXrImiJC7-NSksg3tcPUNRfJCwZQJ URp7A78tEo1KvAE.

Bliss, K. (2017). Eric Clapton on Declining Guitar Sales: 'Maybe the Guitar is Over'. *Billboard*. www.billboard.com/articles/columns/rock/7957989/eric-clapton-guitar-sales-declining-tiff.

Born of Osiris (2011). Behold. On *The Discovery*. Sumerian Records.

Bourdieu, P. (1985). The Market of Symbolic Goods. *Poetics*, **14**(1–2), 13–44.

Bowen, G. (2009). Document Analysis as a Qualitative Research Method. *Qualitative Research Journal*, **9**(2), 27–40.

Brave (2020). How Much Do Twitch Streamers Make. *Brave*. https://brave .com/learn/how-much-money-do-twitch-streamers-earn.

Brooks, C. A. (2012). Chris Brooks Guitar: From Legato to Staccato. *YouTube*. www.youtube.com/watch?v=MswlgtzAH5Q.

Browne, J. (2017). Monuments 'I, The Creator'. *Nail the Mix*. https://members. urm.academy/ntm-sessions/john-browne-monuments.

Buckethead (1996). Robot Transmission. On *Giant Robot*. NTT.

Buckethead (1998). Sanctum. On *Colma*. CyberOctave.

Burns, J. (2016). The History and Future of Amp Modelling. *Philoking*. www .philoking.com/2016/01/28/the-history-and-future-of-amp-modeling (originally accessed 18 Feb. 2021; no longer accessible at time of publication).

Burrell, S. (2020). Jump – Van Halen | Guitar Cover by Sophie Burrell. *YouTube*. www.youtube.com/watch?v=LyZjnXy-ZxQ.

Butterweck, K. (2012). Review of Dragonforce: The Power Within. *Laut.De*. www.laut.de/DragonForce/Alben/The-Power-Within-78262.

Cacophony (1987). *Speed Metal Symphony*. Roadrunner Records.

Campell, R. (2021). Bulletproof Guitar Player. https://bulletproofguitarplayer .com (originally accessed 18 Feb. 2021; no longer accessible at time of publication).

Cheng, W. (2018). So You've Been Musically Shamed. *Journal of Popular Music Studies*, **30**(3), 63–98.

Chopik, I. (2012). Misha Mansoor Interview – Periphery (2012). *Guitar Messenger*. www.guitarmessenger.com/misha-mansoor-interview-periphery-2012.

Citron, M. J. (1993). *Gender and the Musical Canon*. Cambridge University Press.

Click, M. A., Lee, H., & Holladay, H. W. (2013). Making Monsters: Lady Gaga, Fan Identification, and Social Media. *Popular Music and Society*, **36**(3), 360–79.

Cooley, R. (2000). *Shred Guitar Manifesto*. Rusty Cooley.

Cooley, R. (2001). *Extreme Pentatonics*. Rusty Cooley.

Cooley, R. (2002a). *Rusty Rooley*. Lion Music.

Cooley, R. (2002b). Under the Influence. On *Rusty Rooley*. Lion Music.

Copsey, R. (2019). Guitar Music is Thriving, so Why do We Think it's Dying? *Official Charts*. www.officialcharts.com/chart-news/guitar-music-is-thriving-so-why-do-we-think-it-s-dying__25558/.

Corse, S. M. & Griffin, M. D. (1997). Cultural Valorization and African American Literary History: Reconstructing the Canon. *Sociological Forum*, **12**(2), 173–203.

Covet (2016). Nautilus. On *Currents*. Friend of Mine Records.

Covet (2020). Nero. On *Technicolor*. Triple Crown Records.

Custodis, M. (2017). Dream Theater: Komponieren im Virtuosenkollektiv. In T. Phleps (ed.), *Schneller, höher, lauter*. transcript-Verlag, 41–50.

D'Addario (2019). Aaron Marshall (Intervals) – Guitar Power. *YouTube*. www .youtube.com/watch?v=gDXyVeGNrq8.

Dale, P. (2016). *Popular Music and the Politics of Novelty*. Bloomsbury Academic.

Davis, F. (2003). *The History of the Blues*. Da Capo Press.

Dawe, K. (2010). *The New Guitarscape in Critical Theory, Cultural Practice and Musical Performance*. Ashgate.

Deep Purple (1971). Demon's Eye. On *Fireball*. Harvest.

Deep Purple (1972). Highway Star. On *Machine Head*. Purple Records.

Dines, J. (2018a). The Biggest Shred Collab Song in the World II (2018). *YouTube*. www.youtube.com/watch?v=oj0CjV1QxtQ.

Dines, J. (2018b). Shred Wars: Jared Dines VS Jason Richardson. *YouTube*. www.youtube.com/watch?v=-L54r7SXM-8.

Dines, J. (2019). 10 Musicians Play Over the Same Backing Track. *YouTube.* www.youtube.com/watch?v=uzU8xIkaULM.

Doja Cat. (2020). Say So. *YouTube.* www.youtube.com/watch?v=k3Yk6 FrjMkQ.

Dragonforce (2002). *Valley of the Damned.* Noise.

Dragonforce (2012). *The Power Within.* Electric Generation Recordings.

Dream Theater (1994a). *Awake.* EastWest.

Dream Theater (1994b). Erotomania. On *Awake.* EastWest.

Dream Theater (1994c). Voices. On *Awake.* EastWest.

Dunn, S. (2010). Yngwie Malmsteen Interview on his Freakish Obsessions with Guitar. *YouTube.* www.youtube.com/watch?v=2bz6Pk5EsVM.

Ear to The Ground Music (2020). 10 Best Guitarists of this Decade. *Ear to the Ground Music.* www.eartothegroundmusic.co/2020/07/27/10-best-guitarists-of-this-decade.

Edgers, G. (2017). Why My Guitar Gently Weeps: The Slow, Secret Death of the Six-String Electric. *Washington Post.* www.washingtonpost.com/graphics/2017/lifestyle/the-slow-secret-death-of-the-electric-guitar

Electric Sun (1985). *Beyond the Astral Skies.* EMI.

Ellcessor, E. (2012). Tweeting @feliciaday: Online Social Media, Convergence, and Subcultural Stardom. *Cinema Journal,* **51**(2), 46–66.

Espina, E. & Sorenson, T. (2015). *The Milli Vanilli Condition.* Arte Público Press.

Extreme (1990). Get the Funk Out. On *Pornograffitti.* A&M Records.

Fear Factory (1995). *Demanufacture.* Roadrunner Records.

Fellezs, K. (2018). Edge of Insanity: Tony MacAlpine and Black Virtuosity. *Journal of Popular Music Studies,* **39**(1–2), 109–26.

Fernandes, M. G. (2019). Hello Friends. *Instagram.* www.instagram.com/p/B5a3Qd5o7aP (originally accessed 18 Feb. 2021; no longer accessible at time of publication).

Fitterman Radbill, C. (2017). *Introduction to the Music Industry.* Routledge.

Fowler, A. (1979). Genre and the Literary Canon. *New Literary History,* **11**, 97–119.

Friedman, M. (1988). *Dragon's Kiss.* Shrapnel.

Friedman, M. (1992). Tibet. On *Scenes.* Shrapnel.

Friedman, M. (2009). *Tokyo Jukebox.* Mascot.

Frith, S. (2007). What is Bad Music? In S. Frith (Ed.), *Ashgate Contemporary Thinkers on Critical Musicology.* Taylor and Francis, 313–33.

Gambale, F. (1990). New Boots. On *Truth in Shredding.* Tone Center.

Gambale, F. (1992). *Monster Licks & Speed Picking.* Alfred.

Gardiner, J. (2019a). Fake Guitar Playing – It Needs to Stop! *YouTube*. www .youtube.com/watch?v=kc722VQB1EU.

Gardiner, J. (2019b). Jack Gardiner Interview & Mental Health Revisited. *The Guitar Hour Podcast*, 89. https://theguitarhour.libsyn.com/89-jack-gardiner-interview-mental-health-revisited.

Gardiner, J. (2020a). Escapades. https://jackgardinerofficial.bandcamp.com/album/escapades.

Gardiner, J. (2020b). *Escapades*. Self-released.

Gardiner, J. (2021). Mateus Asato Taking a Break is an Important Message for Us All. *YouTube*. www.youtube.com/watch?v=qkJEXWEqJas.

Gatton, D. (1991). Muthaship. On *88 Elmira St*. Elektra.

Genesis (1971). The Musical Box. On *Nursery Cryme*. Charisma.

Geyser, W. (2020). How Much do YouTubers Make? *Influencer MarketingHub*. https://influencermarketinghub.com/how-much-do-youtubers-make.

Gil, V. (2014). Extended Range Guitars (MA thesis). California State University, Los Angeles.

Gilbert, P. (Director) (1995). *Terrifying Guitar Trip*. REH.

Gilbert, P. & Kid, J. (2002). *Raw Blues Power*. Provoge.

Ginsborg, J. (2018). 'The Brilliance of Perfection' or 'Pointless Finish'?: What Virtuosity Means to Musicians. *Musicae Scientiae*, **22**(4), 454–75.

Godin, S. (2008). *Tribes: We Need You to Lead Us*. New York: Portfolio. www .loc.gov/catdir/enhancements/fy0906/2008024978-d.html

Govan, G. (2006a). Hangover. On *Erotic Cakes*. Cornford Records.

Govan, G. (2006b). Sevens. On *Erotic Cakes*. Cornford Records.

Govan, G. (2006c). Wonderful Slippery Thing. On *Erotic Cakes*. Cornford Records.

Griffin, D. J. (2017). Mindful Madness. On *Sentimentality*. Self-released.

Griffin, D. J. (2020). Dan James Griffin. *Patreon*. www.patreon.com/danjames griffin/posts.

Griffin, D. J. (2021). Snowdrift (Single). Self-released.

Grossberg, L. (1992). *We Gotta Get Out of this Place*. Routledge.

Grunwald, A. (2011). Lee McKinney & Jason Richardson Interview. *Guitar Messenger*. https://guitarmessenger.com/lee-mckinney-jason-richardson-interview-born-of-osiris.

Guillory, J. (2010). *Cultural Capital*. University of Chicago Press.

Guitar World (2019). Jason Richardson – Picking Perfection. *YouTube*. www .youtube.com/watch?v=eGnnHvdHwO4.

Guitarwrist (2021). Sophie Lloyd. https://theguitarwrist.co.uk/product-tag/sophie-lloyd.

Halloran, M. & Hearn, E. (2017). YouTube Music. In M. Halloran, ed., *The Musician's Business and Legal Guide*. Taylor and Francis, 78–90.

Hatch, D. & Millward, S. (1987). *From Blues to Rock*. Manchester University Press.

Hearn, E. (2017). Digital Downloads and Streaming: Copyright and Distribution Issues. In M. Halloran, ed., *The Musician's Business and Legal Guide*. Taylor and Francis, 64–76.

Heister, H.-W. (2004). Zur Theorie der Virtuosität. Eine Skizze. In H. von Loesch, U. Mahlert, and P. Rummenhöller, eds., *Klang und Begriff*. Schott, 17–38.

Helfrich, N. (2016). Welcome to The Wasteland. On *Dead Bodies in Motion*. Self-released.

Henabery, J. (1933). *That Goes Double*. Vitaphone Corporation.

Hennion, A. (2012). 'As Fast as one Possibly Can . . . ': Virtuosity, a Truth of Musical Performance. In S. Hawkins and D. B. Scott, eds., *Critical Musicological Reflections*. Ashgate, 125–38.

Henson, T. (2020a). The Making of O.D. *YouTube*. www.youtube.com/watch?v=MZ4QN2uFif8.

Henson, T. (2020b). Tim Henson VS Ichika Nito. *YouTube*. www.youtube.com/watch?v=2wLy9HneuDc.

Herbst, J.-P. (2016). *Die Gitarrenverzerrung in der Rockmusik*. LIT.

Herbst, J.-P. (2017a). Historical Development, Sound Aesthetics and Production Techniques of the Distorted Electric Guitar in Metal Music. *Metal Music Studies*, **3**(1), 24–46.

Herbst, J.-P. (2017b). Shredding, Tapping and Sweeping: Effects of Guitar Distortion on Playability and Expressiveness in Rock and Metal Solos. *Metal Music Studies*, **3**(2), 231–50.

Herbst, J.-P. (2017c). Virtuoses Gitarrenspiel im Rock und Metal. Zum Einfluss von Verzerrung auf das 'Shredding'. In T. Phleps, ed., *Schneller, höher, lauter*. transcript-Verlag, 113–52.

Herbst, J.-P. (2019a). Empirical Explorations of Guitar Players' Attitudes Towards their Equipment and the Role of Distortion in Rock Music. *Current Musicology*, **105**, 75–106.

Herbst, J.-P. (2019b). Old Sounds with New Technologies? Examining the Creative Potential of Guitar 'Profiling' Technology and the Future of Metal Music from Producers' Perspectives. *Metal Music Studies*, **5**(1), 53–69.

Herbst, J.-P. (2023). 'It Just Is My Inner Refusal': Innovation and Conservatism in Guitar Amplification Technology. In A. Moore and G. Bromham, eds., *Distortion in Music Production*. Routledge (174–84).

Herbst, J.-P., Czedik-Eysenberg, I., & Reuter, C. (2018). Guitar Profiling Technology in Metal Music Production: Public Reception, Capability, Consequences and Perspectives. *Metal Music Studies*, **4**(3), 481–506.

Heritage, G. (2016). 'It's Like a Mach Piece, Really': Critiquing the Neo-Classical Aesthetic of '80s Heavy Metal Music'. In A. R. Brown, K. Spracklen, K. Kahn-Harris, and N. Scott, eds., *Global Metal Music and Culture: Current Directions in Metal Studies*. Routledge, 50–67.

Holdsworth, A. (2000). The Sixteen Men of Tain. On *The Sixteen Men of Tain*. Cream Records.

Howe, G. (1988). *Greg Howe*. Shrapnel.

Huron, D. (2007). *Sweet Anticipation*. MIT Press.

Hyatt, A. (2016). Social Media. In A. Macy, C. Rolston, P. Allen, and T. W. Hutchison, eds., *Record Label Marketing*. Focal Press, 215–46.

Ibanez Guitar (2014). James 'Munky' Shaffer from Korn on his Ibanez APEX200 and APEX20 Signature Models. *YouTube*. www.youtube.com/watch?v=zC4_9ojvhNU.

Intervals (2020). 5-HTP. *Circadian*. Sheet Happens.

Jackson, E. A. (2007). Focus – Hocus Pocus Live '73. *YouTube*. www.youtube.com/watch?v=g4ouPGGLI6Q&ab_channel=ElvisAmadeusJackson.

James, R. M. (2007). Deconstruction, Fetishism, and the Racial Contract: On the Politics of 'Faking It' in Music. *The New Centennial Review*, 7(1), 45–80.

Jewlampijs95 (2007). Deep Purple – Wring that Neck. *YouTube*. www.youtube.com/watch?v=Pf7izXdJKrc&ab_channel=Jewlampijs95

Jin, L. (2020). 1,000 True Fans? Try 100. *Andreessen Horowitz*. https://a16z.com/2020/02/06/1000-true-fans-try-100/

John 5 (2005). Fiddlers. On *Songs for Sanity*. Shrapnel.

Johnson, E. (1990). Cliffs of Dover. On *Ah Via Musicom*. Capitol Records.

Jomatami (2020). Tosin Abasi Explains Why He Left Ibanez Guitars & What 'Frustrated Him', Talks 'Hard Lessons'. *Ultimate Guitar*. www.ultimate-guitar.com/news/general_music_news/tosin_abasi_explains_why_he_left_ibanez_guitars__what_frustrated_him_talks_hard_lessons.html.

Jones, C. W. (2017). *The Rock Canon*. Routledge.

Jordan, S. (1988). Stairway to Heaven. On *Flying Home*. EMI.

Keightley, K. (2001). Reconsidering Rock. In S. Frith, W. Straw, and J. Street, eds., *The Cambridge Companion to Pop and Rock*. Cambridge University Press, 109–42.

Kelly, K. (2008). 1,000 True Fans. *The Technium*. https://kk.org/thetechnium/1000-true-fans.

Kennelty, G. (2018). Periphery's Misha Mansoor Says He Can't Make A Living from Just the Band. *Metal Injection*. https://metalinjection.net/its-just-business/peripherys-misha-mansoor-says-he-cant-making-living-from-just-the-band.

Kenner, H. (1984). The Making of the Modernist Canon. In R. von Hallberg, ed., *Canons*. University of Chicago Press, 363–75.

Kermode, F. (1985). *Forms of Attention*. University of Chicago Press.

Korn (1996). *Live Is Peachy*. Epic.

Kotzen, R. (1989). *Riche Kotzen*. Shrapnel.

Kotzen, R., & Howe, G. (1997). *Project*. Shrapnel.

Kraft, J. P. (2004). Manufacturing: Expansion, Consolidation, and Decline. In A. J. Millard, ed., *The Electric Guitar*. Johns Hopkins University Press, 63–87.

Lalaina, J. (2008). Dawn of the Shred. *Guitar World*, **29**(11), 70–4.

Lalaina, J. (2011). Bassist Billy Sheehan Breaks Down Eddie Van Halen's Technique in 1985 Guitar World Interview. *Guitar World*. www.guitar world.com/artists/bassist-billy-sheehan-breaks-down-eddie-van-halens-tech nique-1985-guitar-world-interview.

Lane, S. (2000). *The Tri-Tone Fascination*. Eye Reckon Records.

Larson, T. (2017). Jason Richardson 'Fragments'. *Nail the Mix*. https://mem bers.urm.academy/ntm-sessions/taylor-larson-jason-richardson

Larson, T. (2018). Asking Alexandria 'Into the Fire'. *Nail the Mix*. https:// members.urm.academy/ntm-sessions/taylor-larson-asking-alexandria

Leech-Wilkinson, D. (2018). The Danger of Virtuosity. *Musicae Scientiae*, **22** (4), 558–61.

Leibundgut, Chris (2000). Michael Wagener. Von Wuppertal nach Tennessee, Rock Hard 5/2000, 106–9.

Li, Charmaine (2021). Piano, Guitar, and Healing with Yvette Young. *Pianote*. www.pianote.com/blog/yvette-young-piano.

Little Tybee (2013a). Hearing Blue. On *Distant Viewing*. Paper Garden Records.

Little Tybee (2013b). Left Right. On *Distant Viewing*. Paper Garden Records.

Little Tybee (2016). Languid. On *Little Tybee*. On The Grid Creative.

Lloyd, S. (2020a). Boston – More than a Feeling (Shred Version). *YouTube*. www.youtube.com/watch?v=rEr2JZOa27c.

Lloyd, S. (2020b). Evanescence – Bring Me to Life (Shred Version). *YouTube*. www.youtube.com/watch?v=s50ao6FdIxM.

Lloyd, S. (2020c). How to Play Faster | 3 Notes Per String Scale. *YouTube*. www.youtube.com/watch?v=KqPu-2UyJg4.

Longfield, S. (2017). Tydes. On *Collapse // Expand*. Season of Mist.

Longfield, S. (2020). Lesson Video. *Instagram*. www.instagram.com/p/CGOT-uDgiSJ.

MacAlpine, T. (1985a). *Edge of Insanity*. Shrapnel.

MacAlpine, T. (1987). Hundreds of Thousands. On *Maximum Security*. Shrapnel.

MacAlpine, T. (1985b). Wheel of Fortune. On *Edge of Insanity*. Shrapnel.

Malmsteen, Y. (1984a). Black Star. On *Rising Force*. Polydor.

Malmsteen, Y. (1984b). Far Beyond the Sun. On *Rising Force*. Polydor.

Malmsteen, Y. (1984c). *Rising Force*. Polydor.

Malmsteen, Y. (1990). Demon Driver. On *Eclipse*. Polydor.

Malmsteen, Y. (1996). *Inspiration*. Music for Nations.

Malmsteen, Y. (1999). Blitzkrieg. On *Alchemy*. Dream Dream Catcher.

Mann, L. (2019). Rings of Saturn Lucas Mann 'Fake Guitar' Debunked – Jared Dines Reaction & Response Video. *YouTube*. www.youtube.com/watch?v=5mqYqW7Cnlw.

Marrington, M. (2019). The DAW, Electronic Music Aesthetics, and Genre Transgression in Music Production: The Case of Heavy Metal Music. In R. Hepworth-Sawyer, J. Hodgson, and M. Marrington, eds., *Producing Music*. Routledge, 52–74.

Marten, N. (2018). Guthrie Govan: 'The Older, Wiser Player Knows in a Deep, Intuitive Way that it's the Quality of the Playing that Counts'. *Music Radar*. www.musicradar.com/news/guthrie-govan-the-older-wiser-player-knows-in-a-deep-intuitive-way-that-its-the-quality-of-the-playing-that-counts.

Martin, J. (2015a). Little Tybee's Josh Martin Explains New Guitar Technique. *YouTube*. www.youtube.com/watch?v=elOxW3wbz7A.

Martin, J. (2015b). Little Tybee's Josh Martin 'Glitch Tapping' A Closer Look. *YouTube*. www.youtube.com/watch?v=atGeWypVLxE.

Martin, J. (2017). Josh Martin of Little Tybee – 'Butterfly Tapping'. *YouTube*. www.youtube.com/watch?v=rnxZ%5F1tnCGg%26t=108s%26ab%5Fchannel=LittleTybee.

Martin, J. (2020). Thumping Triads in Harmonic Minor, Melodic Minor, and Harmonic Major! *Patreon*. www.patreon.com/posts/thumping-triads-37753539

Marwick, A. & Boyd, D. (2011). To See and Be Seen: Celebrity Practice on Twitter. *Convergence: The International Journal of Research into New Media Technologies*, **17**(2), 139–58.

Mary (2014). Interview: Aaron Marshall. *Plugin-Mag*. www.plugin-mag.com/interview-aaron-marshall-intervals (originally accessed 18 Feb. 2021; no longer accessible at time of publication).

McAllister, M. (2020). Who is Plini? 'The Future of Exceptional Guitar Playing'. *Produce Like a Pro*. https://producelikeapro.com/blog/who-is-plini-the-future-of-exceptional-guitar-playing.

Metallica (1988). One. On . . . *And Justice for All*. Elektra.

Millard, A. J. (2004a). The Guitar Hero. In A. J. Millard, ed., *The Electric Guitar*. Johns Hopkins University Press, 143–62.

Millard, A. J. (2004b). Heavy Metal: From Guitar Heroes to Guitar Gods. In A. J. Millard, ed., *The Electric Guitar*. Johns Hopkins University Press, 163–80.

Millard, A. J. (2004c). Playing with Power: Technology, Modernity, and the Electric Guitar. In A. J. Millard, ed., *The Electric Guitar*. Johns Hopkins University Press, 123–41.

Minogue, K. (2020). *Disco*. BMG.

Moore, A. F. (2002). Authenticity as Authentication. *Popular Music*, **21**(2), 209–23.

Moore, V. (1986). *Mind's Eye*. Shrapnel.

Moore, V. (1988). Race with Destiny. On *Time Odyssey*. Squawk.

Morris, J. W. (2014). Artists as Entrepreneurs, Fans as Workers. *Popular Music and Society*, **37**(3), 273–90.

Music Ally (2020). Spotify CEO Talks Covid-19, Artist Incomes and Podcasting. *Music Ally*. https://musically.com/2020/07/30/spotify-ceo-talks-covid-19-artist-incomes-and-podcasting-interview.

MyGuitarLessons (2017). Nick Johnston Talks Technique. *MyGuitarLessons*. https://myguitarlessons.co.uk/2017/03/nick-johnston-talks-technique.

Mynett, M. (2017). *Metal Music Manual*. Routledge.

Neely, A. (2020). Can You Play the Mario Kart Lick on Bass? *YouTube*. www.youtube.com/watch?t=327&v=45FtC8OutgI.

Nevermore (2005). Psalm of Lydia. On *This Godless Endevor*. Century Media.

Nito, I. (2020a). 'Sprout' w/ Yvette Young. *YouTube*. www.youtube.com/watch?v=HBDH_YKuprs

Nito, I. (2020b). Runaway. *YouTube*. www.youtube.com/watch?v=BqTjqxLytec.

Nito, I. (2021). Ichika Instagram Lick Tab Series 20 'Melodic Funk'. *Nito Music*. https://nitomusic.bigcartel.com/product/ichika-instagram-lick-tab-series-20-feel-good.

Niu, W. & Sternberg, R. (2006). The Philosophical Roots of Western and Western Conceptions of Creativity. *Journal of Theoretical and Philosophical Psychology*, **26**, 18–38.

Osbourne, O. (1980a). *Blizzard of Ozz*. Jet Records.

Osbourne, O. (1980b). Dee. On *Blizzard of Ozz*. Jet Records.

Osbourne, O. (1981a). Crazy Train. On *Diary of a Madman*. Jet Records.

Osbourne, O. (1981b). *Diary of a Madman*. Jet Records.

Osbourne, O. (1981c). Over the Mountain. On *Diary of a Madman*. Jet Records.

Osbourne, O. (1988). Devil's Daughter. On *No Rest for the Wicked*. Epic.

Owsinski, B. (2016). *A Survival Guide for Making Music in the Internet Age*. Hal Leonard.

Pastukhov, D. (2019). What Music Streaming Services Pay Per Stream. *Soundcharts*. https://soundcharts.com/blog/music-streaming-rates-payouts.

Petrucci, J. (2016). Ernie Ball Music Man Presents: John Petrucci Master Class – Right Hand Warm Up and Picking. *YouTube*. www.youtube.com/watch?v=9UVPBtEFsz8&t=197s&ab_channel=SamAshMusic+5%3A30-5%3A51.

Petrucci, J. (2020). John Petrucci's Guitar Universe 3.0 – July 2021. *YouTube*. www.youtube.com/watch?v=8tgzTu6V0wI.

Plini (2016). Handmade Cities. On *Handmade Cities*. Self-released.

Plini (2019). Plini Shows You How to Build a Complex Riff from a Simple Melody. *Guitar World*. www.guitarworld.com/lessons/building-a-complex-riff-from-a-simple-melody.

Plini (2020a). *Impulse Voices*. Self-released.

Plini (2020b). Q&A. *Instagram*. www.instagram.com/stories/highlights/18167139808011828.

Polyphia (2017). 40oz. On *The Most Hated*. Self-released.

Polyphia (2018a). Nasty. On *New Level New Devils*. Equal Vision Records.

Polyphia (2018b). *New Level New Devils*. Equal Vision Records.

Polyphia (2018c). O.D. On *New Level New Devils*. Equal Vision Records.

Polyphia (2018d). Drown. On *New Level New Devils*. Equal Vision Records.

Provenzano, C. (2018). Auto-Tune, Labor, and the Pop-Music Voice. In R. W. Fink, M. Latour and Z. Wallmark, eds., *The Relentless Pursuit of Tone*. Oxford University Press, 159–82.

Quayle, T. (2020a). Lazy First Finger Syndrome – This is Probably Holding Back your Legato Technique. *YouTube*. www.youtube.com/watch?v=2fcnpwZSXIA.

Quayle, T. (2020b). Lessons. *Tom Quayle*. www.tomquayle.co.uk/lessons.

Racer X (1986). *Street Lethal*. Shrapnel.

Racer X (1987a). Scarified. On *Second Heat*. Shrapnel.

Racer X (1987b). *Second Heat*. Shrapnel.

Racer X (2000). Viking Kong. On *Superheroes*. Universal.

Rage Against the Machine (1992a). Fistful of Steel. On *Rage Against the Machine*. Epic.

Rage Against the Machine (1992b). Killing in the Name. On *Rage Against the Machine*. Epic.

Rage Against the Machine (1996). Bulls on Parade. On *Evil Empire*. Epic.

Recording Academy (2021). Joe Satriani. www.grammy.com/grammys/artists/joe-satriani/17364.

Regev, M. (2006). Introduction. *Popular Music*, **25**(1), 1–2.

Reinhardt, D. (1935 [2016]). Improvisation. On *Monsieur Guitare*. The Viper Label.

RIAA (2021). Van Halen. www.riaa.com/gold-platinum/?tab_active=default-award&se=van+halen#search_section.

Richardson, J. (2016a). Hos Down. On *I*. Self-released.

Richardson, J. (2016b). Omni. On *I*. Self-released.

Rings of Saturn (2019). The Husk. On *Gidim*. Nuclear Blast.

Roche, S. (2021). Mateus Asato Shuts Down Instagram Account, Announces Break From Music. *Guitar World*. www.guitarworld.com/news/mateus-asato-shuts-down-instagram-account-announces-break-from-music.

Ronson, J. (2015). *So You've Been Publicly Shamed*. Picador.

Rotundi, J. (1997). Is Rock Guitar Dead . . . Or Does it Just Smell Funny? *Guitar Player*, **31**(9).

Royce, A. P. (2004). *Anthropology of the Performing Arts*. AltaMira Press.

Sanderson, D. (2020). Kylie Minogue Songwriter Fiona Bevan Paid Only £100 in Streaming Royalties for Album Work. *The Sunday Times*. www.thetimes .co.uk/article/kylie-minogue-songwriter-fiona-bevan-paid-only-100-in-streaming-royalties-for-album-work-xbdl0cxcs.

Satriani, J. (1986a). *Not of this Earth*. Relativity.

Satriani, J. (1986b). The Snake. On *Not of this Earth*. Relativity.

Satriani, J. (1987a). Midnight. On *Surfing with the Alien*. Relativity.

Satriani, J. (1987b). Satch Boogie. On *Surfing with the Alien*. Relativity.

Satriani, J. (1987c). *Surfing with the Alien*. Relativity.

Satriani, J. (1989a). Flying in a Blue Dream. On *Flying in a Blue Dream*. Relativity.

Satriani, J. (1989b). The Mystical Potato Head Groove Thing. On *Flying in a Blue Dream*. Relativity.

Sawtooth World (2020). Michael Angelo Batio Sawtooth Double Guitar Performance at NAMM 2020 w ChromaCast String Dampener. *YouTube*. www.youtube.com/watch?v=8VzoTQveX-A.

Scallon, R. (2014). For That Second. On *Anchor*. Self-released.

Schmidt-Horning, S. (2004). Recording: The Search for the Sound. In A. J. Millard, ed., *The Electric Guitar*. Johns Hopkins University Press, 105–22.

Scorpions (1976). *Virgin Killer*. RCA Victor.

Scorpions (1977). The Sails of Charon. On *Taken by Force*. RCA Victor.

Seth, L. (2017). Dragonforce Guitarist Shoots Down Accusation Band Speeds Up Its Songs in The Studio. *Blabbermouth*. https://blabbermouth.net/news/ dragonforce-guitarist-shoots-down-accusation-band-speeds-up-its-songs-in-the-studio

Sheet Happens (2020). Sheet Happens Publishing. www.sheethappenspublishing .com.

Shelvock, M. (2014). The Progressive Heavy Metal Guitarist's Signal Chain: Contemporary Analogue and Digital Strategies. *KES Transactions on Innovation in Music*, **1**(1), 126–38.

Shred Guitar TV (2019). Guitar Lesson: Rusty Cooley – Arpeggio Madness 1. *YouTube*. www.facebook.com/watch/?v=411973850004417

Slaven, J. E. & Krout, J. L. (2016). Musicological Analysis of Guitar Solos from the Roots of Rock Through Modern Heavy Metal. *Metal Music Studies*, **2**(2), 245–51.

Stachó, L. (2018). Mental Virtuosity: A New Theory of Performers' Attentional Processes and Strategies. *Musicae Scientiae*, **22**(4), 539–57.

Standards (2020). Special Berry. On *Fruit Island*. Topshelf Records.

Steeler (1983). *Steeler*. Shrapnel.

Strachan, R. (2017). *Sonic Technologies*. Bloomsbury Academic.

Strohm, J. (2004). Women Guitarists: Gender Issues in Alternative rock. In A. J. Millard, ed., *The Electric Guitar*. Johns Hopkins University Press, 181–200.

Swift, T. (2017). Look What You Made Me Do. On *Reputation*. Big Machine Records.

Symphony X (1997). Of Sins and Shadows. On *The Divine Wings Of Tragedy*. Inside Out Music.

Talbot, M. (2000). Introduction. In M. Talbot, ed., *The Musical Work*. Liverpool University Press, 1–13.

Théberge, P. (1997). *Any Sound You Can Imagine*. Wesleyan University Press.

Todd, L. (2019). Fake Shredders – Hot Take. *YouTube*. www.youtube.com/ watch?v=yucPd0n9hfg.

Tolinski, B. (2017). *Play it Loud*. Anchor Books.

Toneforge (2020). Jason Richardson. https://joeysturgistones.com/collections/ toneforge/products/toneforge-jason-richardson.

Total Guitar (2012). Paul Gilbert Guest Lesson – String Muting. *YouTube*. www .youtube.com/watch?v=53yX_0XnZrc.

Turner, G. (2015). Electric Guitar Performance Techniques (PhD thesis). University of Sheffield, Sheffield.

Vai, S. (1984). *Flex-Able*. Food For Thought Records.

Vai, S. (1990a). Ballerina 12/24. On *Passion and Warfare*. Relativity.

Vai, S. (1990b). *Passion and Warfare*. Relativity.

Vai, S. (1995a). Bad Horsie. On *Alien Love Secrets. R*elativity.

Vai, S. (1995b). Tender Surrender. On *Alien Love Secrets*. Relativity.

Vai, S. (1998). *Alien Love Secrets*. Image Entertainment.

Vai, S. (2004). *Steve Vai's Guitar Workout*. Hal Leonard.

Vai, S. (2010). Ibanez Universe 20th Anniversary Reissue. *YouTube*. www .youtube.com/watch?v=RsELKt_nquQ.

Vallejo, A. P. (2020). *Development, Mechanics and Compositional Uses of Virtuosic Electric Guitar Techniques* (MA thesis). University of Huddersfield, Huddersfield. http://eprints.hud.ac.uk/id/eprint/35522.

Van Halen (1978a). Ain't Talkin' 'Bout Love. On *Van Halen*. Warner Bros.

Van Halen (1978b). Eruption. On *Van Halen*. Warner Bros.

Van Halen (1978c). I'm the One. On *Van Halen*. Warner Bros.

Van Halen (1979). Spanish Fly. On *Van Halen II*. Warner Bros.

Van Halen (1981). Mean Street. On *Fair Warning*. Warner Bros.

Van Halen (1982). Cathedral. On *Diver Down*. Warner Bros.

Waksman, S. (1999). *Instruments of Desire*. Harvard University Press.

Waksman, S. (2003). Contesting Virtuosity: Rock Guitar Since 1976. In V. Coelho, ed., *The Cambridge Companion to the Guitar*. Cambridge University Press, 122–32.

Waksman, S. (2004). California Noise: Tinkering with Hardcore and Heavy Metal in Southern California. *Social Studies of Science*, **34**(5), 675–702.

Walser, R. (1992). Eruptions: Heavy Metal Appropriations of Classical Virtuosity. *Popular Music*, **11**(3), 263–308.

Webster, J. (1959a). Caravan. On *Webster's Unabridged*. RCA Victor.

Webster, J. (1959b). Fountain Mist. On *Webster's Unabridged*. RCA Victor.

Wiederhorn, J. (2015). Shrapnel Records: The House That Shred Built. *Louder Sound*. www.loudersound.com/features/shrapnel-records-the-house-that-shred-built.

Weinstein, D. (2013). Rock's Guitar Gods: Avatars of the Sixties. *Archiv Für Musikwissenschaft*, **70**(2), 139–54.

Weissman, D. (2017). *Understanding the Music Business*. Taylor and Francis.

Wendell, H. V. (1991). Canonicity. *Modern Language Association*, **106**(1), 110–21.

Wenger, E. (1998). *Communities of Practice*. Cambridge University Press.

Werner, A. (2017). YouTube and Music Video Streaming: Participation, Intermediation and Spreadability. In S. Johansson, A. Werner, P. Åker, and G. Goldenzwaig, eds., *Streaming Music*. Taylor and Francis, 138–56.

West, K. (2016). *Champions*. Def Jam Recordings.

Whiteley, S. (1990). Progressive Rock and Psychedelic Coding in the Work of Jimi Hendrix. *Popular Music*, **9**(1), 37–91.

Williamson, J., & Cloonan, M. (2013). Contextualising the Contemporary Recording Industry. In L. Marshall, ed., *The International Recording Industries*. Routledge, 11–29.

Wood, G. D. (2010). *Romanticism and Music Culture in Britain, 1770–1840*. Cambridge University Press.

Wylde, Z. (1996). 1,000,000 Miles Away. On *Book of Shadows*. Geffen Records.

Xavier, T. (2015). Plini Interview. *Gear Gods*. https://geargods.net/interviews/australia-week-plini-interview.

Yngwie J. Malmsteen's Rising Force (1998). Blitzkrieg. On *Alchemy*. Dream Catcher.

Young, Y. (2020). Patience Riff. *YouTube*. www.youtube.com/watch?v=6Mt0lMW1fCw.

Zappa, F. (1976). Black Napkins. On *Zoot Allures*. Warner Bros.

Popular Music

Rupert Till
University of Huddersfield

Rupert Till is Professor of Music at the University of Huddersfield, UK, Associate Dean International in his faculty and Director of the Confucius Institute at the University. He has research interests in popular music and sound archaeology. He is Chair of the International Association for the Study of Popular Music IASPM, and a committee member of the UK and Ireland Branch. He directed Huddersfield activities within the EU funded European Music Archaeology Project, (2013–18), and has been Principal Investigator for two AHRC/EPSRC grants. He studied composition with Gavin Bryars, Christopher Hobbs, Katharine Norman, and George Nicholson. He continues to write electronica and perform under the name "Professor Chill".

About the Series

Elements in Popular Music showcases exciting original work from across this lively, diverse and expanding field. It embraces all aspects of popular music studies, from music history and ethnomusicology to composition, songwriting and performance, and the music industries, recording and production. Its content will also appeal to scholars and students of media studies and cultural studies exploring topics such as fandom, celebrity, screen studies and music journalism. The study of popular music often involves crossing disciplinary boundaries and drawing on a variety of empirical and creative methodologies to illuminate topics such as identity and embodiment, power and resistance. Each Element in the series is illustrated by engaging case studies that will attract a broad range of readers from the academy and beyond.

Cambridge Elements ☰

Popular Music

Elements in the Series

Rock Guitar Virtuosos: Advances in Electric Guitar Playing, Technology And Culture
Jan-Peter Herbst & Alexander Paul Vallejo

A full series listing is available at: www.cambridge.org/epop